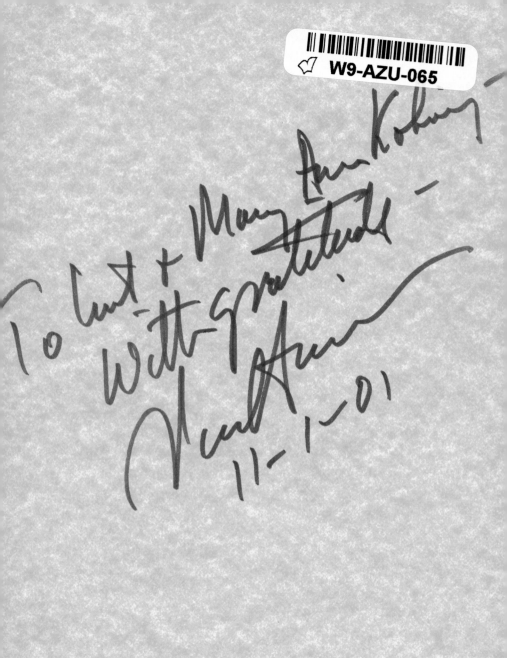

To Curt + Mary Ann Koteng

With gratitude –

Neal Armstrong
11–1–01

❧ Freedom's Champion

Freedom's Champion ᠗ Elijah Lovejoy

Paul Simon

With a Foreword by Clarence Page

Southern Illinois University Press
Carbondale and Edwardsville

Library of Congress Cataloging-in-Publication Data

Simon, Paul, date.
    Freedom's champion—Elijah Lovejoy / Paul Simon : with a
foreword by Clarence Page.
        p.   cm.
    Rev. ed. of: Lovejoy, martyr to freedom. 1964.
    Includes index.
        1. Lovejoy, Elijah P. (Elijah Parish), 1802–1837.   2. Abolition-
ists—Illinois—Alton—Biography.   3. Riots—Illinois—Alton—
History—19th century.   4. Alton (Ill.)—Biography.   I. Simon,
Paul, date. Lovejoy, martyr to freedom.   II. Title.
    F549.A4L72   1994
    973.5'092—dc20
    [B]   93-45581
    ISBN 0-8093-1940-3   CIP
    ISBN 0-8093-1941-1 pbk.

To Howard Metzenbaum,

like Elijah Lovejoy, a courageous
champion of opportunity and justice

We don't need to do anything to history
to make it better, sexier, happier, safer,
more relevant. We need only listen to it,
accept it, even in its seemingly unbearable
moments, and trust in its lessons.
—Ken Burns, filmmaker and
producer of "The Civil War"

Contents

ɜ&

Illustrations

Foreword

Ever since Paul Simon published a shorter book on the martyred abolitionist Elijah P. Lovejoy in 1964, the two seemed to me to be an appropriate match. Both built formidable reputations as teachers, humanitarians, and crusading editorial writers. Simon's reputation came quite early. Long before the nation got to know him as a U.S. senator and a 1988 candidate for the Democratic presidential nomination, Simon, at nineteen, took over what would eventually be a chain of thirteen southern Illinois newspapers. He immediately embarked on a relentless crusade against local gangsters and machine politicians, a battle that carried considerable risks with it, just as Lovejoy's crusade against slavery proved fatal for him and his printing presses. Like Lovejoy, Simon, the son of a Lutheran minister, is closely associated with sober Yankee virtues of hard work and charity, a virtually spotless reputation that helped him get elected to the Illinois General Assembly in 1954 despite opposition from party regulars, to the state Senate in 1963, to lieutenant governor in 1966 (the only to be elected while the other party won the governorship), to the U.S. House of Representatives in 1975, and to the U.S. Senate in 1984.

In a political age of breathtaking scandals and rampant cynicism, Simon stands out among friends and foes alike in his trademark bow ties and monotone voice as refreshingly modest and dull. His idea of a "wild time," a congressional colleague once quipped, is "dinner and a discussion of history."

Indeed, Simon has continued to study history and write about it even as he was making it. He has written more than a dozen books and hundreds of weekly newsletters to constituents, but with this book, he touches on a subject of particular interest to me, as an editorial writer, a transplanted Illinoisan, and a great-grandson of African American slaves. Like other students of journalism history, I have long been fascinated by Lovejoy. His tenacity brought him tremendous hardship and eventually an early death, yet he persevered simply on principles whose persuasive force was energized by his death, stirring a ground-swell that brought the great slavery debate to a head and brought the country to civil war.

I have long wondered, what manner of man was Lovejoy? Why was he not content to edit newspapers, operate the school he founded, and quietly worship his God? Why did he refuse to ease up his crusade against the abominable institution of slavery in St. Louis, in a slave state, when a number of important men signed a letter in 1835 asking him to moderate the tone of his editorials? Why, after threats forced him to move across the Mississippi to the free state of Illinois, did he persevere even after his press was destroyed several times in one year? Why did he fight on until the night of November 7, 1837, when he died defending his press from a mob? Was he a zealot, a radical revolutionary, a religious fanatic, a madman, or a visionary motivated by what Martin Luther King, Jr., called a "divine dissatisfaction"?

I think Paul Simon has performed a great service by shedding valuable light on these questions. He has uncovered a compli-cated man whose restless spirit and single-minded, religiously fired idealism showed many characteristics, some of them more noble than others. Simon shows Lovejoy to be a less-than-perfect hero. It is not entirely clear how much he outgrew some of the religious prejudices and insensitivities of his time and place, particularly against Roman Catholics. But, in his finer moments,

Lovejoy answered to a higher power in promoting the highest ideals of equal opportunity for all to pursue life, liberty, and happiness in an open marketplace of ideas.

As all great biographies should, this book tells a story not just about a man but also about his times. As such, it sends an important message across the decades to offer valuable insight into the social and political conflicts of our own times and the qualities needed by any individuals who would set out to move the giant canyon walls of history. As Frederick Douglass, an escaped slave who rose to become a leading abolitionist, diplomat, and pioneer African American journalist, used to say, a man cannot hold down another man without holding himself down as well. With that in mind, Lovejoy can be remembered as a man who helped free slave and slaveholder alike to help Americans rise to a higher state of humanity and offer a brighter guiding light to the world.

A monument to Lovejoy stands in Alton, Illinois, as a landmark of American journalism and an enduring symbol of the power the right words can have to trouble the public conscience, move people to action, and subvert unjust ideas and practices that others might think to be immovable. A monument is one type of memorial. This book is another.

Clarence Page

Preface

Few people accomplish great things during the course of their lives. They do what society expects of them, but beyond their immediate families, they do not change the lives of others significantly.

This is the fascinating story of a man who lived less than thirty-five years and changed history.

Elijah Lovejoy loved God and humanity in a way that had meaning in his life. A syrupy, smooth, comfortable religion, which called for no more sacrifice than a weekly offering, was not for him. His faith marched.

He also believed in freedom. He meshed his religious life with the cause of freedom—freedom of the press and freedom for African Americans.

This is not the story of a perfect man. You will see his weaknesses as well as his strengths, but like the prophets of old, Lovejoy is remembered for the positive things he accomplished.

His was a life of days filled with service, not of years filled with emptiness; a life of heart, not hate; a life of faith, not fear.

I could wish no finer destiny for anyone.

An earlier biography of Lovejoy, which I wrote for a teenage audience, published by Concordia Publishing House in 1964 and long out of print, became the basis for this substantially expanded and more thoroughly researched biography.

As in any dramatic event, accounts of those involved are sometimes contradictory, not from malicious intent, but from differing recollections. Where that is the case, I have used the account that is the most probable action, either because more people recalled it that way, or because of the authenticity of the source, or because other circumstances suggest its greater reliability.

Since this book was designed for the reading of the general public rather than as a document of historical research, certain liberties were taken in quotations: *grog-shop* became *tavern*, for example. Archaic terms and phrases were changed; punctuation was altered for readability; grammatical errors were corrected. In no instance was the intent of the original quotation changed, but the researcher who wishes to be exact should go to the source material.

Acknowledgments

I am grateful to the library staffs who have helped in my research: Cheryl Pence, George Heerman, Jennifer Ericson, Janice Petterchak, Linda Oelheim, and Cheryl Schnirring at the Illinois State Historical Library; Charles Brown at the St. Louis Mercantile Library; Patience-Anne W. Lenk át the Miller Library, Colby College, Waterville, Maine; Theresa McGill, Linda Evans, and Ralph Pugh at the Chicago Historical Society Library; Barbara Stole at the Missouri Historical Society Library; Charlene Gill at the Alton Museum of History and Art; David Tilghman, Joan Higbee, Clark Evans, Abe Boni, Bob Costenbader, Larry Boyer, and Aggree McPhatten Jackson at the Library of Congress; and John Abbott at the Lovejoy Library, Southern Illinois University at Edwardsville.

Special recognition is due the Wickett-Wiswall Collection of Lovejoy Papers in the Southwest Collection of Texas Technological University, Lubbock, Texas. Other helpful sources have been materials at the Missouri Historical Society Library, the Illinois State Historical Library, the Library of Congress, St. Louis Mercantile Library, the Huntington Library in Pasadena, California, the Chicago Historical Society Library, the Newberry Library in Chicago, the Colby College Library, and the William L. Clements Library at the University of Michigan, as well as others, all supplying helpful additional details.

I am grateful to those who read the rough draft of the manuscript and helped in other ways: my wife, Jeanne; my brother, Rev. Arthur Simon; Judy Wagner; Robert Tabscott; Minnesota State Senator John Marty; David Carle; and Christopher Ryan. As in any such volume, the mistakes and errors of judgment are mine, not theirs.

A number of people helped with information that added important detail to the book, such as Richard Forstall of the Population Division of the Bureau of the Census. They are not all listed here, but I am grateful to them.

Jackie Williams has once again labored amazingly well through my written notes and the words I pounded out on a manual typewriter.

I am also grateful to earlier Lovejoy biographers, Merton Dillon and John Gill.

Among those who have helped to preserve the Lovejoy legacy are three who died in recent years, Jesse Cannon, Paul Cousley, and Burton Bernard, and one who is still living, Irving Dilliard.

Deserving of special commendation for exceptional work to keep the Lovejoy legacy, traditions, and goals alive are the people at Colby College and Rev. Robert Tabscott, a St. Louis Presbyterian minister, who has produced a film about Lovejoy and has been both an effective scholar and a promoter of the martyr.

My thanks also to Rev. William G. Chrystal and Phillip G. Dow, Sr., and to those at Southern Illinois University Press who took an interest in this project: Kenney Withers, Dave Gilbert, Howard Webb, and Carol Burns.

Freedom's Champion

ह 1

ह From Maine to the Frontier

On November 9, 1802, in a small Maine village, Elizabeth Lovejoy gave birth to a boy who would be buried by a few frightened friends on his birthday thirty-five years later. His name: Elijah Lovejoy. The village: Albion, Maine, forty miles inland from the Atlantic Ocean. The 1810 Census lists Albion Township (then called Fairfax) at a population of 924. You would hardly expect this peaceful hamlet to produce a man whom people would hate and persecute and finally kill, nor would you expect this quiet town to be the birthplace of a man whose death would electrify the nation.

Elijah Lovejoy's father, born in the year of the Declaration of Independence, was Rev. Daniel Lovejoy, a Congregational minister who also farmed. Rev. Francis Lovejoy, Elijah's grandfather, also served as a Congregational minister, a descendant of John Lovejoy, who emigrated from England in 1635 at age thirteen to what is now Massachusetts. A great uncle, Abiel Lovejoy, served as a representative in the Assembly of the state of Massachusetts Bay. Elijah's family lived in a wooden house on land his grandfather had cleared. The sloping, timbered land joined what became known as Lovejoy Pond, which has a shoreline of approximately five miles. Here all the Lovejoy children received their first strong lessons in right and wrong, as well as in the ABCs.

The first of nine children (seven boys and two girls), Elijah learned about the decision his father had made as an uneducated nineteen-year-old farm boy to leave the fields and become a

1

minister. The elder Lovejoy went to a small academy in Byfield, Massachusetts, and stayed at the home of a Congregational minister, Rev. Elijah Parish, well-known in England for his religious leadership and for his support of the Federalists. Daniel Lovejoy felt deeply indebted to the minister, and when his firstborn son came, he named him Elijah Parish. Throughout Elijah's life, his family almost always called him Parish.

Stern in the religious training he gave to his nine children, Daniel Lovejoy found that his rigid demeanor sometimes caused him problems. Moody, he was not able to get along with everyone. At seventeen, he experienced "a session of deep mental distress."[1] Sometimes as an adult, he became extremely depressed. His family knew this, as did those who heard him preach. At one point, he wrote to Elijah that a letter he had received from his son "found me in a state of deep mental debility, to which as you know I have always been more or less subject."[2] Elijah referred later to "those fits of morbid melancholy" his father had.[3] After the death of one of his sons, Daniel Lovejoy, Jr., the father wrote: "I wondered why God would not [spare] his precious life. . . . It seemed hard that he must be taken from me. It seemed as if it was more than I could bear and I looked forward to death for relief."[4] Today he would be diagnosed as a manic-depressive. At the funeral of the senior Lovejoy, the eulogy included these significant words that would also apply to his son Elijah: "As he was ardent and decided in his feelings, he did not always, perhaps, exert that conciliating influence which one of a different temperament would have done." And in the midst of his words of praise for the deceased, the eulogist also noted: "He was subject to an unnatural elevation and depression of spirits."[5]

Because of his moody nature, the senior Lovejoy received a variety of smaller preaching assignments rather than a lengthy stay at any one congregation. Typical of his assignments were three months of missionary work among the Indians and a twelve-week period when he furnished "moral and religious instruction to the poor and destitute."[6] His instructions on working with the Indians are of interest because of Elijah's later activities: "As you will be called to mingle with Christians of different denominations, while you stedfastly [sic] maintain the discipline of the Congregational churches, treat all who differ from you with kindness and candour. . . . You will cautiously avoid taking a part in political controversies."[7] Daniel Lovejoy died in 1833, at the age of fifty-eight, four years before the death of his son Elijah shook the nation.

Elijah's mother, Elizabeth Patee Lovejoy, was emotionally more stable and as fully devoted to Christian living and serving the cause of her faith as her husband. She read widely, including some of the more difficult theological books. The mood swings of her husband and the death of three sons before Elijah's death were reflected in her somewhat gloomy theological outlook. A gentle but powerful force in the intellectual and spiritual growth of the nine Lovejoy children, she wrote occasional letters to her oldest son that would mean much to him in later years when he faced danger. At one point, Elijah wrote to his sister Sybil about their mother: "I have never seen her equal, take all her qualities together. So pure, so disinterestedly benevolent a heart seldom lodges in a house of clay."[8]

By the age of four, black-haired and dark-eyed little Elijah could read the Bible, a skill taught him chiefly by his mother. He memorized more than one hundred hymns. Attendance at the public school increased his hunger for books. He read everything he could get at the local library or among his father's theological books, and he loved poetry. The two things his youthful friends remembered best about him were that he was an unusually bright student and an unusually good athlete. Five feet nine inches tall and muscular, he combined natural physical ability with something else that makes a good athlete: courage. This quality eventually would make him famous. One friend described him as having "a round pleasant face."[9] In most respects, he had a normal youth for someone in the new United States. He enjoyed swimming—he was the best swimmer in the area—did his share of plowing, and fished with his grandfather.

In September 1823, shortly before he turned twenty-one, Elijah entered Waterville College (now Colby College) in Maine, a small Baptist-supported school. Because he was immediately recognized as a superior scholar, the administration arranged for financial help to permit him to complete his college work. The school president, Rev. Jeremiah Chaplin, believed the hardworking student to be a genius.

The religious atmosphere of Elijah's childhood continued to influence his college years. A residence at which he stayed on a vacation while attending college distressed him. He thought the woman of the household, a relative, "was as little qualified to educate a family as any person I was ever acquainted with." There were several boarders at the place, and he found himself disgusted "by their shocking profanity and intemperance."[10] His mother wrote to him: "I fear much for your health lest you apply yourself too [diligently] to your studies and impair your constitution." She added: "We beseech you and plead with you to make God your friend, to be reconciled to God, to make Christ your refuge."[11] Throughout the years, correspondence between Elijah Lovejoy and his parents dwelt heavily on religion.

During Elijah's childhood, his parents had stressed the necessity of religious conversion, believing that some singular experience was necessary for a person to be a Christian. Elijah, already a little on the moody side during his college years, worried because he had not experienced the dramatic conversion he wanted. He continued to read every theological book he could find, but the more he read, the more he wanted the conversion about which he had learned at home. Because he could not honestly tell anyone of such spiritual lightning hitting him, he described his life as miserable, and his parents were also movingly unhappy.

A typical letter from his father started: "I have felt more than usually concerned of late for the salvation of my children."[12] In one letter, the twenty-one-year-old college student Elijah wrote his father: "There have been moments even in my short existence, when to have become a nothingness would have been embraced by me. But those were dreadful moments. I cannot describe them. If I know my own heart, I do now feel the necessity of resigning myself into the hands of my God, to mould and guide me at His will; tho I dare not say that I am, at present, willing to do it. All that I know and all that I feel is that religion is important, that I do not possess it, and that without it I am miserable indeed." He added: "I should choose that no one else [in the family] should see [this letter]."[13] He wrote poetry to help relieve his mind of difficulties. To add to his problems, he fell in love, and the woman would not have him.

At twenty-three, Elijah graduated from Waterville College at the head of his class. He spoke at the commencement, giving a fairly typical student graduation speech: "When we are treading the devious and to us untried paths of life, the time that we have passed in this seat of learning will be to us a source of unqualified enjoyment." For graduation, he also wrote a poem, "Inspirations of the Muse." A spirit of freedom pervades the poem, in which he describes the mind as "free and unshackled as the viewless wind."[14] Nevertheless, Elijah's high scholastic standing gave him little satisfaction. Later he described himself in another poem:

Of all that knew him, few but judged him wrong;
He was of silent and unsocial mood;

Unloving and unloved he passed along,
His chosen path with steadfast aim he trod,
Nor asked nor wished applause, save only of his God.[15]

Before leaving college, he had to pay an additional thirty-four cents for library services, presumably for books not returned promptly. After college, Lovejoy tried a year of teaching in the nearby town of China, Maine, but it did not challenge him enough. He decided to head westward to the nine-year-old state of Illinois. A combination of adventure, new opportunities, and patriotism prompted those on the eastern seaboard to do what Horace Greeley advised citizens to do in later years: "Go west, young man."

Upon leaving Maine, Lovejoy wrote a poetic tribute "of a swelling heart" to the area. His poem included these lines that reflect both his thoughts and the poetic style of the time:

Thy sons are noble, in whose veins there runs
A richer tide than Europe's kings can boast,
The blood of freemen: Blood which oft has flowed
In freedom's holiest cause; and ready yet to flow,
If need should be; ere it would curdle down
To the slow sluggish stream of slavery.[16]

This isolated reference to slavery—perhaps meaning only breaking the shackles from Europe's royalty—does not indicate any significant interest by Lovejoy in the issue of slavery at this point. His poetry and other writings suggest a young man more attuned to theology than any political issue, adventuresome and, as he described himself, "unswayed by love, and unrestrained by fear."[17] And there is an uncommonly frequent reference in his writings to death.

Lovejoy mapped his course: south to Boston, then to New York City, and then west to Illinois. At Bath, Maine, twenty-four-year-old Elijah Parish Lovejoy took a boat for Boston. He kept a diary to record the details of the hardships of his trip. Storms and strong winds prevented a normal, short passage between the two cities, and he found himself "sick, sick, sick." The enthusiastic young Lovejoy noted that the boat in which he traveled was, in his words, "taken from the British in the last war and as I gazed upon her and thought of the glorious achievements of my countrymen, my heart beat thick and proudly."[18] The sight of the exciting city of Boston, his first view of a "big city," made him forget his seasickness. At the outset, Lovejoy thought he would earn some money before heading westward, but for five days he looked for a job unsuccessfully. Almost out of money, he finally decided to walk to Illinois!

Walking to Illinois from Boston by way of New York City— twelve hundred miles—would have been hard enough if he had had money and if the land to be covered was settled. Besides the physically difficult job of walking so many miles, Lovejoy faced the question of how he would eat and the perceived peril of being attacked by animals, particularly when sleeping. In the western portion of his trip, he also considered the possibility that he might meet Indians who, unhappy with the abuse they had taken from whites, might take revenge on a young white man traveling alone. Having come directly from the physically soft life of a teacher, he found that the long hiking gave him much pain. He was often depressed, and these aches, plus frequent headaches and the need to keep going with little food, made him all the more wretched. For June 1, 1827, he recorded in his diary: "I am now 250 miles from home, in a land of strangers and but 80 cents in my pocket." Three days later, he pawned his watch for five dollars. On Sunday, June 4, 1827, he passed through Ware, Massachusetts, and attended church services conducted by a Rev. Cook. In a foretaste of the future Lovejoy, the brash young traveler sent him a letter: "Your delivery was too hurried, too indistinct and unvaried. . . . In general, it seemed as if your eloquence 'played round the head but comes not from the heart.' "[19]

After several weeks, he finally reached his first major stop, New York City. He tried to get a job in order to make a few dollars and to take a rest from his long hiking. The job he finally secured consisted of walking around New York City selling newspaper subscriptions. But this gave him money only for living, not saving for his trip further west. Finally, he made contact with Jeremiah Chaplin, the president of Waterville College, which he had attended. Chaplin, who thought highly of Lovejoy, took pity on him and lent him some money. Lovejoy wrote in his diary: "May the God of the wretched reward him ten thousand fold."[20] The money made the rest of the trip easier. He now could afford rides on boats and wagons between his walking expeditions. For a time, he had to stop in western New York because of malaria, but he recovered quickly. After his illness, or perhaps during it, he penned a poem about himself entitled "The Wanderer," which included these lines:

> . . . now had he come
> To the far woods, and there in silence knelt
> On the sharp flint-stone in the rayless gloom,
> And fervently he prayed to find an early tomb.[21]

He ended his journey in Hillsboro, Illinois, at the home of John Tillson, a friendly Presbyterian who made Lovejoy feel comfortable in his big house, the largest in Montgomery County. But Hillsboro, Illinois, in 1827 had no demand for a teacher or a college graduate. Illinois had been settled from the south to the north. Chicago was one of the smallest Illinois towns. Finding a place that needed a teacher meant going to the state capital, Vandalia; to the thriving city of Shawneetown in deep southern Illinois; to the rapidly growing river city of Alton; or to the big frontier town of St. Louis in Missouri. For a man who had walked all the way from Boston, walking seventy-five miles from Hillsboro to St. Louis posed no problem. Lovejoy packed his few belongings and headed for St. Louis.

Eight years after its founding by the French in 1764, St. Louis had a population of 399 whites and 198 slaves. In 1821, six years before Lovejoy arrived there, Missouri had been admitted to the Union as a slave state, part of the famous Missouri Compromise. Under this compromise, fashioned by Henry Clay, Missouri was admitted as a slave state, but future states were to be admitted as free, assuring the gradual national decline of slavery.

Five years before Lovejoy arrived, the Missouri legislature had incorporated St. Louis, a city with a population of 5,600. Late in 1827, when Lovejoy came, the population exceeded 6,000, a tremendous population for the frontier West. After all the small villages and the wilderness Lovejoy had been through, St. Louis seemed like a huge metropolis. Fur trade was the big business, although agriculture and river traffic also were major factors in the growth of St. Louis. Lovejoy saw these things, and he saw the influence of many national groups: the French, Spanish, English, and Irish, plus smaller numbers from other ethnic groups. He also saw the big stone auction block near the river where slaves were sold, but there is no evidence that this particularly impressed him.

Unlike in Lovejoy's native New England, organized religion had little influence in the frontier town of St. Louis. Here he found no Congregational church. The rough-and-tumble atmosphere of St. Louis and his doubts about his Christian conversion meant that religion did not dominate his life as his parents hoped, though he wrote to them: "We have in this place a very able Presbyterian minister and a most respectable congregation and it is evidently becoming more fashionable (to say nothing [of] those who attend from better motives) to go to church in this city."[22] His religious upbringing and New England background were still part of him. Many things happening in St. Louis—the drunkenness, the profanity, the open immorality—he disliked and did not want to share.

At this time, neither Missouri nor Illinois had public schools, and Lovejoy thought that teaching, starting his own school, would be a way to make a living and to bring some "good New England culture" to St. Louis. Surprisingly, his school became a success. It did not change the life of St. Louis to any great degree, but he influenced a number of young people, and he found himself rather popular, a pleasant experience that he would never have again. His mother wrote to him, finding herself "gratified . . . that your school is so highly spoken of in the [Missouri] Republican." She also said that she prayed "that you may be preserved from the many temptations and vain allurements . . . of this ensnaring but deceptive world."[23]

Lovejoy's school did well financially. Not only did he send money home to Maine, he also saved for himself and lived well, according to St. Louis frontier standards. In his letters home, he wrote of an "abundance of room yet" in St. Louis and on the frontier until they have "the civil and religious privileges with which New England is blessed."[24]

However, Elizabeth Lovejoy was not happy with her oldest son being so far away on the frontier. She had heard many stories about life in St. Louis, and most of the unpleasant stories were true. It did not seem like a good place for her son, and she wrote: "You say I might have anticipated the time when my children would leave me. So I have. But I cannot see any necessity why they should go so far from me. What special call have you 2,000 miles from your parents?"[25] About this time, a poem entitled "My Mother" appeared in the *Missouri Republican*, published in St. Louis, which has all the earmarks of being authored by Lovejoy and which his brothers later believed he wrote:

    . . . I am far away
    From home, and love, and thee:
    And stranger hands may heap the clay
    That soon may cover me.[26]

Just as Lovejoy found teaching in the small community in Maine not challenging enough, so after two years of teaching in St. Louis he again became dissatisfied. His chance to make a change came: he bought a half interest in the *St. Louis Times* and became the new editor. His name first appeared in the *Times* on August 14, 1830, and for the last time as editor on February 18, 1832. Just below the front page masthead, *St. Louis Times*, on the left-hand side of the page appeared the words: "By Lovejoy and Miller." T. J. Miller, facing financial problems, had sold a half interest in the newspaper to Lovejoy. Frequent changes in editors and publishers were common during this period of U.S. history, particularly in areas of more scattered population.

Editing a newspaper at this time required not only the ability to write but also the ability to fight. Newspaper editors said exactly what they thought of public officials and other citizens, and it was common for a newspaper editor to meet an opponent on the street and to end up badly beaten. Editors called each other names in print that many today would not use even in conversation. Lovejoy's chief rival newspaper in St. Louis, the *St. Louis Beacon*, called him a "little animal" and accused him of not paying his employees.[27] Lovejoy replied in the next issue of the *Times* that the charge was not true and that the editor of the *Beacon* was "a mere inflated bladder." The *Richmond Enquirer* called Lovejoy a "contemptible parasite."[28]

These were times when people spoke in extremes and when tolerance was rare. Lovejoy, a Henry Clay supporter, sometimes went along with the spirit of that period and wrote strong anti-Jackson opinions, which in later years no responsible newspaper would have published. His letters to his family in New England showed this same intolerance. After Andrew Jackson's inauguration as president, for example, he referred to him in a letter as "an adulterer and [a] murderer" who had "fools and knaves for his advisers."[29]

But aside from the strong stands and commentaries on national issues and local congressional races, Lovejoy's newspaper would not have won any journalistic prizes or attracted much interest, except for reflecting the culture of that day: someone set up a small steam engine and some rails at the Old Baptist Church, and Lovejoy rode on it "attended with no pain."[30] The election for mayor of St. Louis resulted in 383 votes cast. And one other small news item would play a role in his future: "The Rev. Edward Beecher of Park Street Church, Boston, has been chosen President of the new College in Jacksonville, Illinois. We doubt his acceptance of the proposed honor."[31]

The advertisements also reflected the times. One firm advertised "city made hats" from New York City.[32] The firm of Vairin and Reel announced they had "4 barrels Alcohol and 10 barrels Cherry Bounce just received and for sale."[33] And occasionally, there was an unusual advertisement: "For six days only. Mr. Cops begs leave to inform the Ladies and Gentlemen of St. Louis that he intends presenting his Anaconda—also called Boa Constrictor—with a live Rabbit on Monday the 13th June at 5 o'clock P.M. Admittance 50 cents."[34]

But Lovejoy's political comments did cause excitement. In fact, two prominent men died in a duel because of articles in Lovejoy's newspaper. The *Times*, mostly concerned with Whig politics and little else, took a strong stand against Congressman Stephen D. Pettis, seeking reelection. One of the big issues throughout the nation was whether there should be a national bank. President Jackson opposed it, and Congressman Pettis supported Jackson. Major Thomas Biddle, a brother of U.S. Bank president Nicholas Biddle, lived in St. Louis. Newspaper comments on the bank issue, including those in Lovejoy's *Times*, stirred passions. This was particularly true of Congressman Pettis and Major Biddle, and soon Congressman Pettis challenged the major to a duel, not uncommon in those days.

Nearsighted, Major Biddle said he could accept the challenge only if they fought the duel with pistols just five feet from each other. And that is the way they fought. Lovejoy—who had helped cause the conflict—wrote the day after the duel: "We regret to add that both gentlemen are dangerously wounded. Major Biddle is shot through the abdomen, the ball lodging within. Mr. Pettis is shot through the side just below the chest, the ball passing through the entire body. We understand that the conduct of both parties on the ground was entirely honorable." He added that the two entered the duel with "coolness and courage."[35]

In the next issue, Lovejoy reported that both had died, although he devoted much more space to Major Biddle, whom he had favored in the political quarrel, than to Congressman Pettis. He praised them, however, and noted that "both gentlemen suffered the most excruciating pain from the time of their being wounded till their death." He condemned "false notions of honor" that caused the duel and said that he hoped he would "never again witness such a tragedy."[36] The issue two weeks later contained a poem against dueling.

Little in the *Times* indicated that in a few years Lovejoy would become famous for his stand against slavery. He gave more attention to the St. Louis Association for the Improvement of the Breed of Horses than the slavery issue. Slavery did not merit attention either in the editorials or in the news comments. Small notices about meetings on Colonization—an effort to send slaves back to Africa—appeared, as did one news item about action by the Louisiana legislature "prohibiting slaves from coming into the state, or departing, with any traveller."[37] Except for those small items and the advertisements, a reader would not have guessed that slavery presented either national or Missouri problems any more than in a nonslave nation like England.

The advertisements in the *Times* were like those in any newspaper in a slave state. The newspaper advertised slaves for sale, and the *Times* office of Lovejoy even became a clearinghouse for trade in slaves. Here are typical advertisements:

FOR SALE—A first rate NEGRO MAN, about 22 years of age. Apply at this office.

SALE OF NEGROES by Auction at Lane & Co.

FOR SALE—A likely NEGRO WOMAN with six children. The woman is between 30 and 35 years of age, and the two oldest children, twins, are between 10 and 11 years old. They will be sold for CASH. Apply at this office.

FOR SALE—A likely mulatto boy in his 16th year, accustomed to cooking and sundry other house business, of good character. For terms enquire of Col. Coleman at the Land Office.

30 DOLLARS REWARD—Ranaway . . . a negro named JOHN. He is about 5 feet high, well proportioned, and has a large dent across his nose. . . . I will give for apprehending the above negro $10 if taken in St. Louis, $20 if in the State of Missouri, and $40 if taken in the State of Illinois and delivered to Mr. L. Deaver, St. Louis, or secured in any jail so I can get him again.

AUCTION SALE—[begins with a list of merchandise including an Italian clock, breakfast and card tables, and silverware] a Negro Girl, about 14 years of age. She is a good nurse and washer.

FOR SALE—A Negro Woman. 28 or 30 years of age, a first rate washer and ironer, a native of Missouri (title indisputable). For further particulars, enquire at this office.

AUCTION—A likely Negro Woman, about 40 years of age, an excellent Nurse and House servant.

$20 REWARD. Ranaway . . . a Negro Boy named Bob, about 14 years of age. . . . Had on a fur cap, the fur much worn off; he has 4 double teeth, 2 in the upper and 2 in the lower jaw; a scar on his Leg. . . . When interrogated, he speaks so fast as to almost stutter.

NOTICE IS HEREBY GIVEN that we will expose to the highest bidder, on Monday, 9th of May next . . . at the residence of Thomas South, a likely NEGRO BOY, named Harrison, about 7 or 8 years old.[38]

There were also advertisements for "Negro Clothes," loose-fitting and coarse materials that the slaves wore.

That slaves were not as happy as their white masters liked to pretend is clear from the number of advertisements in Lovejoy's newspapers for runaway slaves:

> $20 Reward. Ran away on Sunday evening, a bright Mulatto Man named Claibourne, about 25 years of age, six feet high, stout made, a very bright Mulatto, his teeth rather broad, has a down-cast look when spoken to. He took with him a broad cloth coat half worn, patched under the arm. . . . He can read a little, and is supposed to have forged free papers and to be making his way to Canada.[39]

In the East, William Lloyd Garrison was stirring interest in what became known as Abolitionism, immediate freedom for slaves. Garrison published the *Liberator*, a weekly newspaper that stimulated discussion of the issue. Some of Lovejoy's family accepted Abolitionist beliefs, but Lovejoy thought that anyone favoring these ideas did a disservice to the country. His brother Joseph displeased him by becoming an agent in Maine for Garrison's *Liberator*.

Unlike the Abolitionists, the American Colonization Society favored a gradual approach to eliminating slavery. Organized with the intention of sending the slaves back to Africa as free men and women, it was composed partially of people who felt slavery wrong, but who did not feel so moved that they wanted to free all slaves in the United States immediately. Others in the group were not particularly hostile to slavery but feared the presence of African Americans in their midst, particularly free African Americans. In a sense, the Colonization Society was a compromise between the supporters of slavery and the Abolitionists, and individual citizens and religious groups contributed millions of dollars for the cause. Lovejoy showed mild interest in the St. Louis branch of the American Colonization Society. But slavery held no great importance for him. More important was whether Jackson or Clay would be president and who would lead the St. Louis political scene.

For a period, at least one slave worked in the office of Lovejoy's newspaper. His name was William — later called William Brown. In a few years, he escaped to freedom in Canada where he wrote a brief autobiography in which he told of hearing his mother being whipped and of his own growing to adulthood as a slave. He had a few lines about Lovejoy:

> I was soon taken from Mr. Colburn's, and hired to Elijah P. Lovejoy, who was at that time publisher and editor of the "St. Louis Times." My work, while with him, was mainly in the printing office, waiting on the hands, working the press, etc. Mr. Lovejoy was a very good man, and decidedly the best master that I had ever had. I am chiefly indebted to him, and to my employment in the printing office, for what little learning I obtained while in slavery.

While living with Mr. Lovejoy, I was often sent on errands to the office of the "Missouri Republican," published by Mr. Edward Charles. Once, while returning to the office with type, I was attacked by several large boys, sons of slaveholders, who pelted me with snowballs. Having the heavy form of type in my hands, I could not make my escape by running; so I laid down the type and gave them battle. They gathered around me, pelting me with stones and sticks, until they overpowered me, and would have captured me, if I had not resorted to my heels. Upon my retreat, they took possession of the type; and what to do to regain it I could not devise. Knowing Mr. Lovejoy to be a very humane man, I went to the office, and laid the case before him. He told me to remain in the office. He took one of the apprentices with him, and went after the type, and soon returned with it; but on his return informed me that Samuel McKinney had told him that he would whip me, because I had hurt his boy. Soon after, McKinney was seen making his way to the office by one of the printers, who informed me of the fact, and I made my escape through the back door.

McKinney not being able to find me on his arrival, left the office in a great rage, swearing that he would whip me to death. A few days after, I was walking along Main Street, he seized me by the collar, and struck me over the head five or six times with a large cane, which caused the blood to gush from my nose and ears in such a manner that my clothes were completely saturated with blood. After beating me to his satisfaction, he let me go, and I returned to the office so weak from the loss of blood, that Mr. Lovejoy sent me home to my master. It was five weeks before I was able to walk again. During this time it was necessary to have some one to supply my place at the office, and I lost the situation.[40]

Soon Lovejoy's attitude toward slavery would undergo a radical change that would result in his own death and a shock to the nation.

৶ 2

৶ Editor, Preacher, and Fighter

People who knew Lovejoy in St. Louis considered him rather straitlaced, and many would have been surprised to learn that he belonged to no church. However, the influence of a strong religious upbringing was part of his daily living, and his comfortable life did not appear to call for any revolutionary changes. Not wealthy, he still lived well compared with most of the population. The *St. Louis Times* enjoyed increased advertising and circulation, which was reflected in Lovejoy's lifestyle.

The *Times* encouraged religious activities, whether by a local church or by the new societies that were coming to the frontier to promote Bible reading, tract distribution, Sunday school work, and temperance in drinking. Lovejoy joined the Missouri and Illinois Tract Society, which fostered the distribution of religious literature. It was the only group with which he affiliated, and he became the recording secretary. When a man came to St. Louis to speak against religion, Lovejoy attacked him in a *Times* editorial.

Lovejoy went to hear various evangelists and religious leaders when they visited St. Louis, but none made any significant dent in his semi-active commitment to religion. We know from his letters home that although he belonged to no church, he went to church regularly. He also made occasional editorial comments that indicated religious interest. Once Lovejoy wrote in his newspaper: "We know not how it may be in the Episcopal and Methodist Churches of the City; but in the Presbyterian Church, the singing is absolutely intolerable."[1] He suggested that the choir's singing might be appreciated more by dogs than by people.

A year after he became editor of the *Times*, Lovejoy attended revival meetings in the First Presbyterian Church. The 1831 religious revival sweeping the country reached the frontier city of St. Louis. He attended these nightly services regularly and wrote to his parents that he had prayed to be converted. They joined in that prayer, but at the end of the series of services, Lovejoy was not among the converts. This disappointed both him and his parents. More and more, he lost interest in religion.

Word from his parents of the death of his younger brother Daniel in February 1831 added both to Lovejoy's sense of melancholy and to a renewed interest in religion. He asked his parents to pray for his conversion and added: "It seems to me scarcely possible that one who has so long lived in sin, who has resisted so much light, and has so often grieved away the Holy Spirit, as I have, should be again visited with its heavenly influences."[2]

In January 1832, the same church held another series of revival meetings. Many regarded the guest preacher, Rev. David Nelson, as one of the ablest speakers in the West. Men, women, and children crowded into the warm church from the cold outdoors and in candlelight heard Dr. Nelson condemn sin with vigor. As members of a rugged frontier society, the people who gathered to hear Dr. Nelson understood what he meant. This minister not only attacked sin in a general way but also pinpointed it. One of the sins he brought to life before his hushed audiences was slavery. He made them see that God condemned the sale of human beings taking place in their city and state. For one person to own another was, he charged, in the eyes of God, a sin as great as adultery or murder. Dr. Nelson moved his audiences. During this series of revivals, there were more than twice as many converts — sixty-six — as during the revival services the previous year. Elijah Parish Lovejoy became one of the converts.

Most who read his letters and writings today would regard Lovejoy as already a Christian and his "conversion" more of a dedication to greater religious practice, for although he had not had the emotional experience that he hoped for and that many expected, he did accept the traditional Christian beliefs. However, after his conversion, he wrote his parents: "I was, by divine grace, enabled to bring all my sins and all my sorrows, and lay them at the feet of Jesus, and to receive the blessed assurance that He had accepted me, all sinful and polluted as I was. . . . I made a public profession of religion, and joined the church in this city." Then he added: "Brother Owen and brother John, you are now the only members of the family . . . who have not made your peace with God. . . . Tempt not God, as I have done. Think of poor brother Daniel, and make your peace with a Saviour before you sleep, after reading this."[3]

Whether it is called a conversion or a dedication, it had a profound effect on Lovejoy's life and ultimately on the nation's life. Dr. Nelson had no idea of the eventual impact he made on either the man or the nation when he noted among his converts at the First Presbyterian Church a young newspaper editor named Lovejoy.

Elijah's parents were tremendously pleased. His mother called it "just what I have prayed for with all my heart." It was particularly meaningful to his mother because of Elijah's younger brother's unexpected death. His mother said Daniel's death "overwhelmed me with gloom and despondence."[4] His father, also pleased at the conversion, said that Elijah praised his parents too much for giving him a religious background. "You gave us more credit than we think we deserve," he wrote.[5]

At that time, conversion meant more than simply a statement of faith and regular church attendance. It meant changing the whole direction of life, and it included an agreement to help change the lives of others. For his part, Lovejoy experienced great uncertainty as to what to do with his newly changed life. He felt strongly that he should not continue as a newspaper editor. He talked with Rev. William Potts, pastor of the First Presbyterian Church of St. Louis, and on his advice decided to become a minister. When Lovejoy's brother Joseph heard the news, he wrote to his parents: "This news must have been like cold water to a thirsty soul to your fainting spirits. . . . More than this we may not expect in this world."[6]

Lovejoy acted quickly. Within two weeks, he sold his share of the *St. Louis Times*. The February 18, 1832, edition contained his farewell message to his readers. He explained that "circumstances most unexpected" and "of a personal character" had forced him to withdraw from the paper. He enjoyed his work as editor even though he found the job difficult. He left the position with no hard feelings toward anyone, "whether friend or foe." He included a religious message in which he pointed out that without "the religion of the Bible neither civil nor intellectual freedom can long exist." The next week the new editors explained: "The former editor retired from his office from causes and reasons which had nothing to do with the concerns of the paper."

In March 1832, at the age of twenty-nine, Lovejoy enrolled at Princeton Theological Seminary in New Jersey, where most Presbyterian ministers were trained. He did not know that he had made his last trip to the East. When the summer recess arrived, Lovejoy returned to Maine for his last visit there. He went home, rather than continuing his studies through the summer, because his father was having "fits of morbid melancholy." Always easily depressed, Daniel Lovejoy worsened. In one letter, Lovejoy refers to his father as having "a mind diseased."[7] By this time, three of the nine Lovejoy children had died, and this weighed heavily on his father. The death of Daniel, the son named after him who died after heavy drinking, particularly touched him. It was more than the sad-natured father could bear, and his severe mental problems returned temporarily. When Elijah went home for his summer visit, he found his mother holding up well under all the strain.

While visiting in Maine, Lovejoy did a little preaching in area churches and then headed back to Princeton. As brilliant a student at the seminary as he had been in college, he completed his training in thirteen months. He wrote regular letters to his family while at Princeton and never mentioned the issue of slavery. His correspondence testifies to his belief that God has carved out the future for all of us, which we have little ability to change. When the first child of his brother Joseph died at the age of two, Elijah wrote from the seminary: "I most sincerely console with you on the affliction which it has pleased God to send you. . . . If you could see what God sees you would heartily discern that what has been done is best for both you and the child."[8] That attitude of passive acceptance of fate would partially change in the next four years. His letters showed a preoccupation with his personal religious life and with that of his family but almost nothing about how his faith might be applied to life.

Licensed to do his practice preaching in the Philadelphia area, Lovejoy went from there to Newport, Rhode Island, for several weeks, and then to the Spring Street Church in New York City for a few months. He thought about returning to Maine to be near his parents, but all these places had only limited appeal. As a pastor, he could have had a comfortable life working in the East. Word of his high scholastic standing spread among the clergy, and they regarded him as a minister with a bright future. But in Lovejoy's thinking, the area that really needed to have Christianity preached to it was the West. In addition, the predominantly Protestant nation viewed the West as a battleground between Protestants and Catholics, and anti-Catholic prejudice was a major force on the American religious scene.

Lovejoy planned to make a trip from New York to Maine to spend time with his parents when he received an important message from St. Louis. A group of Protestant businessmen, among them a future governor of Missouri, Hamilton Rowan Gamble, resolved to start a newspaper in St. Louis that would promote religion, morality, and education. Looking for an editor who knew how to run a newspaper and who either was a minister or had some prestige among the ministry, they felt that such a man could do much to change the sinful ways of St. Louis. The man who had this combination of talents was Elijah Parish Lovejoy, and it took no time to convince him to return to the frontier. The businessmen offered him twelve hundred dollars to buy the press and equipment. Lovejoy would have complete control of editorial policy. If in any year the net income exceeded five hundred dollars, the surplus would be paid to the investors.

Before he accepted the offer, Lovejoy wrote to his parents who wanted him to stay in New England: "If my dear Parents request me to stay in New England, I will do it."[9] But the tone of the letter made it virtually impossible for them to object. Three weeks later, by the time the senior Lovejoy already had been buried, Elijah learned of his father's death. A man of limited means and abilities, Daniel Lovejoy had lived long enough to see his son prepare for the ministry.

A young man named Andrew Benton had actually tried to get a religious newspaper underway in St. Louis two years earlier, had issued some announcements about it, and had stirred some interest, but Benton did not have the right combination of talents and financial backing to get it going, and the task fell to Lovejoy. Elijah wrote his brother Owen: "They are impatiently calling me to the West, and to the West I must go."[10] In a letter to his mother he said: "Duty appears plainly to call me West. . . . I do not by any means give up the expectation of seeing you again. If I live I shall probably be eastward in a year or two at farthest."[11] Lovejoy felt the needs in St. Louis so pressing that he decided to return there immediately rather than go to Maine to visit his mother. Before Lovejoy left New York, the American Home Missionary Society commissioned him to preach for them among the scattered churches on the Missouri frontier, and he planned to combine this evangelistic work with his editing. Lovejoy arrived in St. Louis on November 12, 1833, three days after his thirty-first birthday. Not a person to move slowly, he published his first issue of the *Observer* ten days later; it was the first Protestant religious newspaper west of the Mississippi. On its masthead were the words: "Jesus Christ, and Him Crucified." In an opening message to his readers, Lovejoy said he had "the hope that it will succeed in obtaining the good will of all before whom it may appear," but he also said it would support "a system of religious doctrines to which it will inflexibly adhere." No hint of future involvement in the issue of slavery appeared in Lovejoy's newspaper at this point. The contents showed this to be basically a religious newspaper. A typical issue carried articles on "Original Sin," "The Missionary Enterprise," "A Revival Scene," "Report of the Fourth Annual Meeting of the Illinois Sunday School Union," and smaller news items about religious activity in the nation.[12] A Philadelphia newspaper noted that it was "as well printed as any of our Eastern periodicals."[13] However, the *Observer* had few advertisements — very few compared with the other St. Louis newspapers. Because advertising is a newspaper's main source of income, the early issues indicated that Lovejoy would eventually run into financial trouble.

Although the *Observer* carried occasional references to slavery, the first enemies its editor made were not due to his articles on slavery but rather to his religious presentations. In the 1830s, the public had strong opinions on matters of religion, if they had any opinions at all. Rumors and emotion combined to make people do and say strange things in the guise of faith. Lovejoy was intolerant of those who did not share his Presbyterian beliefs, and there were not many Presbyterians in St. Louis, though their numbers were growing. Particularly intolerant of Roman Catholics, he did not simply disagree with them on certain doctrines; he condemned anyone associated with the Roman Catholic Church. Since Lovejoy's extreme opinions were characteristic of the age in which he lived, his fellow Calvinists of that day would not have viewed them as extreme. He published strongly anti-Catholic letters signed by "Waldo," but more than that, he editorially expressed deep prejudices himself in a community that numbered one-third Catholics. In the midst of articles with topics such as "Disuse of Tobacco," his anti-Catholic diatribes appeared, a typical one beginning: "Popery is spreading in our country to an alarming degree, and this too entirely by foreign influence and . . . foreign money."[14]

While Roman Catholics were his number one target, he took out after other groups as well, including Baptists and Campbellites, later known as Disciples of Christ. He also attacked the Church of England and, by implication, Episcopalians. But initially Lovejoy ran a fairly dull newspaper, except for those who were close followers of the religious and theological scene. Nevertheless, St. Louisans did not appreciate his vituperative Presbyterian lectures. What part this may have played in the final drama is difficult to know. Lovejoy could have made and kept friends by stating his views more tactfully. At the very least, he silenced people who otherwise might have come to his defense.

However, Lovejoy did not confine his writing to religious matters, and many other items and comments appeared in the *Observer*:

DESERVED PUNISHMENT

A fellow has been lately sentenced to an imprisonment of four months at New Haven, for having insulted females on the street.

The drawing of lotteries and sale of lottery tickets ceased in New York on the 26th of December. When will they cease here?

On Monday last a woman without arms was married at Bury, the ring being placed by the bridegroom upon one of the bride's toes.

It is difficult for persons living in the older countries to realize the rapidity with which towns and villages spring into existence in the West. Chicago is situated near the northeastern extremity of Illinois. Last spring there were in Chicago five or six streets, now there are from 20 to 25; then there were 150 inhabitants, now from 800 to 1,000.

TOBACCO

A young man of our acquaintance has foolishly addicted himself to the practice of chewing this filthy weed.

Public executions are injurious to the morals of a community.

JACKSONVILLE COLLEGE

We had the pleasure of attending the late Commencement at this Institution. There were no graduates, as the college has not been in operation long enough.[15]

These excerpts provide a bit of the flavor of the newspaper Lovejoy published. Some items were strange, some humorous, but most fell into neither category—like the lengthy articles about technical theological subjects, such as transubstantiation, that could not have interested many in St. Louis.

Illness plagued Lovejoy, and for several issues he could not serve as editor. He then returned, "though still with trembling hand."[16] Another time he wrote in the *Observer*: "We have put the above article together with the fever rioting in our veins, the headache holding high jubilee in our temples."[17]

Running a newspaper with little advertising had its practical difficulties. After eleven months in business, Lovejoy wrote: "There are now due to us from subscribers several hundred dollars, for the want of which we are most seriously embarrassed. By their conduct they are endangering the very existence of the *Observer*."[18] A month later, he pleaded his case again: "The *Observer* is today a year old. The paper — and it need not be disguised — is in a very precarious condition. It is in debt, and is getting [deeper] into debt every week. Now this state of things cannot continue much longer."[19] Another issue indicated he received no salary.

The Illinois Presbyterian Synod voted to encourage subscribers to the *Observer* because of the "importance of a religious periodical" and the financial "embarrassments of the establishment."[20] Lovejoy wrote Rev. John Brooks of Belleville, Illinois: "The object of this letter is to inquire if you can do anything to help along the 'Observer'. It is now sinking money at the rate of $30.00 per week. Unless a united effort is made on the part of those who feel an interest in its success, it cannot go on. . . . We have no subscribers in your church or neighborhood. If the ministers do not take hold, nothing can be done. Can you do anything? Will you try?"[21] Lovejoy's appeals met with some success, for the paper continued, and soon there was an advertisement: "WANTED — An apprentice to the printing business, one who can come well recommended, from 12 to 15 years of age."[22]

In the midst of all his business difficulties, Lovejoy started to take a stand on the issue of slavery. He did it quietly at first, usually by quoting a comment from some other newspaper or magazine. Seven months after the first *Observer* appeared, he offered editorial comment comparing the relative stands of the Abolitionists, who favored immediate freedom for the slaves, and the Colonizers, who favored buying their freedom and sending them to the colony of Liberia in Africa. Lovejoy supported the Colonizers, and on the question of whether slavery is wrong, he simply commented in a sentence buried in the midst of a long discourse: "Our laws are unjust in the heavy load of disabilities which they impose upon the colored man."[23]

A statement that appeared in his former newspaper, the *St. Louis Times*, prompted his first strong stand. The *Times* called for mob action against a few women who had started a Sunday school for slaves. While Lovejoy made it clear that he was not an Abolitionist, he sided squarely with the women who taught the slaves. "Bind their bodies in whatever chains you please," he wrote, "they have souls as precious as those of their masters." The idea that slaves should not be taught religion, as the *Times* suggested, he found "monstrous" and "horrible." That paper's attitude was "shameful" and "savage," he said. As to teaching religion, his answer was simple: "God commands it."[24]

Approximately a year later, Lovejoy published an article, signed simply "N," which attacked the institution of slavery and which was written by a former slaveholder who had released his slaves. Lovejoy wrote that he agreed that slavery is wrong, but added: "We do not believe that this change ought to be immediate and unconditional emancipation. We are entirely convinced that such a course would be cruel to the slave himself, and injurious to the community at large."[25] In the same editorial, he commended the *Missouri Republican* for its support of a political move for a state constitutional amendment that would have permitted all slaveholders to keep their slaves but would have prohibited future or additional ownership of slaves. Two weeks later, he called upon Christians owning slaves to look after the slaves' religious welfare. "Many professed Christians habitually treat their slaves as though they had no immortal souls, and it is high time such a practice as this were abolished."[26]

Gradually, Lovejoy's positions became firmer and more militant. He shifted from being concerned only about saving the souls of the slaves to confronting the issue of slavery itself. In an editorial published July 21, 1834, he finally decided that "slavery as it now exists among us, must cease to exist."

Two touching articles, probably involving the same man, appeared. Lovejoy quoted in part from the *Missouri Republican*, also published in St. Louis. A man "purchased a negro woman, under the following circumstances. She was about 24 years old, of excellent character, and married to a husband about 28 years of age. As soon as the bargain was closed the driver told her to start, giving her only ten minutes to prepare. She was not allowed to see her husband. She, however, sent him word that she was gone, and bade him good-bye. . . . When the poor fellow, her husband, heard the message he seemed absolutely stunned with the most unexpected blow. He followed his poor wife to town to take a last look, but the thought of parting was more than he could bear." He tried to escape. When they caught him, they "first flogged him severely, but finding the wretched man not sufficiently sensitive, they took him out into the woods and, laying him across some rails, they inflicted the blows with a saw on his bare back and shoulders. The poor man was then corded to a board for the night, and the next day chained." Lovejoy noted that though this man's "face is not as white, his blood is as red and as warm as your own."[27]

After a year, it was common to read in Lovejoy's paper about "the groans of the wretched," "lacerated bodies of helpless men, and women, and children," and "weeping mothers torn from helpless babes."[28] In another commentary, he wrote: "The atmosphere of slavery is an unnatural one for Americans to live in. The institution is repugnant to the very first principles of liberty."[29] He noted in an editorial, printed in italics so it would stand out, that there is "a great and a very criminal apathy of feeling among the Christians of Missouri, as it respects the condition of our slaves."[30]

However, in all of this, he repeatedly made clear that he was not an Abolitionist but that he favored a gradual solution to the problem. "The example of England is showing us that gradual abolition is safe, practicable and expedient," Lovejoy wrote.[31] He called those seeking immediate freedom for the slaves "unwise, inconsiderate, and headstrong."[32] When a group of women in the East announced that they would start a paper urging the freeing of the slaves, Lovejoy editorially called their action "unwise."[33] Another time, he said that Abolitionists are "devoid alike of pity, of humanity, and of shame."[34] When he discovered that his brother Joseph in Maine was an Abolitionist, he wrote to him: "I regret, deeply regret, that you cannot see the true effect of all such measures." He told his brother that those who ask for immediate freedom for slaves "are riveting the very chains you seek to break." He added: "You have never lived in a slave state. . . . You cannot have any just conceptions of the relation existing between master and slave. It is bad enough—too bad—but it is not as you think. [William Lloyd] Garrison—I seldom permit myself to write the name—knows better. He has been in a slave state, and he is therefore a dishonest man. How can you hold communion with such a foul-mouthed fellow?"[35] Lovejoy's differences with Garrison centered not only on the latter's advocacy of the immediate abolition of slavery but also on his hostility toward organized religion, particularly the clergy.

As objective as he considered himself to be, Lovejoy nevertheless lived in the culture of a slave state. However, most people in Missouri wanted no one to favor even gradual freedom for slaves. His occasional references to slavery being bad upset people; he received mail asking why he did not "let a certain subject alone." Lovejoy responded: "We do let it alone whenever it is possible so to do. But sometimes it is not possible."[36] Actually, by comparison with other subjects, he did not mention slavery frequently during the first year and a half of his work. He spent much more time denouncing "Popery" and "Sabbath-trampling, mission-hating Baptists."[37]

When a mob destroyed a combination tavern, gambling house, and house of prostitution, he sounded a warning that would soon be significant: "In this particular case of Monday night, the end accomplished was a good one — a den of drunkenness and impurity was broken up, a public nuisance was abated. But this was done in an illegal manner; and it surely is a most incongruous method of vindicating the laws, by trampling on them ourselves. . . . Who is secure in life or property if the laws are placed at the mercy of a phrensied [*sic*] rabble?"[38] Almost every issue carried warnings of the dangers of drinking — though the same issues carried wholesale prices on wine in St. Louis. Tobacco also continued to be an object of attack. In one issue, he announced a "declaration of war against this filthy, poisonous, nauseating, noxious, foul, pestiferous weed."

In addition to his editorial duties, Lovejoy preached and did work with religious societies that took him around the state. On one of these trips, he met an attractive young woman, Celia Ann French, from St. Charles, Missouri. On March 4, 1835, Rev. William S. Potts, the Presbyterian pastor who had persuaded Lovejoy to enter the ministry, married them. Lovejoy wrote to his mother describing his wife as "tall, well-shaped, of a light, fair complexion . . . large blue eyes . . . she is pious. . . . She is, I know, intelligent, refined, and of agreeable manners; and unless I have entirely mistaken her character, she is also sweet-tempered, obliging, kind-hearted, industrious, good-humoured, and possessed alike of a sound judgment and correct taste. . . . In addition to all this, she loves me."[39] She was twenty-one; he was thirty-two. Their married life would be exciting — and short.

More and more, Lovejoy publicly supported freedom for the slaves. A few months prior to being married, Lovejoy had attended a meeting of the Presbyterian Synod of Missouri and had placed himself among the minority who took an open stand against slavery. The Presbyterians of the St. Louis area had commissioned him as an evangelist, and when he went about the area preaching, he concentrated on the need for religious conversion, outlining in colorful detail the sins being committed and giving attention to slavery. Moreover, with almost every issue, his newspaper used plainer language in discussing slavery. When the editor of a New Orleans religious newspaper announced he would permit no more discussion of slavery in his publication, Lovejoy wrote in an editorial: "If the Christians of Louisiana and Mississippi cannot bear the discussion of this subject, they may as well give up their religious newspaper altogether."[40] Yet he still wrote that he did not favor immediate freedom for all slaves. He wanted them to be freed gradually, and he opposed slaves running away from their masters.

However, the talk in the streets made no fine distinctions between those who were for gradual freedom and those who favored immediate freedom. Lovejoy's stance made him an Abolitionist in the eyes of most people, and they regarded that as an explosive stand, one that would destabilize their society. One of the top officers in the First Presbyterian Church in St. Louis visited Lovejoy frequently during the summer following his marriage and urged him to stop writing about slavery. He said that Lovejoy placed himself in real danger of action by a mob. Others also counseled this, but Lovejoy continued on the same path.

In September 1835, Lovejoy went to a religious "camp meeting" near Potosi, Missouri, a town approximately sixty miles from St. Louis. Word had spread ahead of Lovejoy about his views on slavery, and what he said at the meeting stirred the situation even more. His return schedule to St. Louis called for passing through the town of Potosi during the afternoon. When this became known, two men decided that they would waylay Lovejoy in order to tar and feather him: cover his body with hot tar, put chicken feathers on the tar, and then display him. Lovejoy knew nothing of the plot, but at the last minute, he changed his plans and did not leave until the following morning. The two men, tired of waiting, gave up the idea. Lovejoy learned about their plan on his way to St. Louis. Upon arriving there, he discovered that a handbill had been circulated, urging mob action to destroy the *Observer*. "The *Missouri Argus* openly called upon the hurrah boys to mob me down," Lovejoy wrote his brother Joseph.[41] If this frightened Lovejoy, it did not show in his newspaper; he continued on the same course.

To add to the tension of the situation, Lovejoy, in his capacity as a representative of a Bible Society, sent Bibles to Jefferson City, Missouri, and he needed papers to pack around the Bibles. Presumably without giving it a second thought, he used some old copies of the *Emancipator*, a New England antislavery newspaper, for that purpose. At that point, Lovejoy neither subscribed to an Abolitionist newspaper nor exchanged his newspaper with one, but apparently he had been given a few copies of the militant publication, which he stuffed inside the box to fill space not occupied by the Bibles. At least that is Lovejoy's account. When the box containing the Bibles was opened in Jefferson City, the antislavery papers caused an uproar. Lovejoy assured his readers that the *Emancipator* was not "regularly or generally received at this office. . . . I am assured that had I been in the city at the time, I should surely have suffered the penalty of the whipping post or the tar-barrel, if not both! I understand that a Christian brother was one of those who brought the report here from Jefferson City, and was among the most active in circulating it, and declaring his belief in my criminality."[42] A friend immediately wrote urging him to "act with caution." The situation is so tense, said this friend, that when people opened the box and discovered the antislavery literature, someone could have "blown up a blast with but little encouragement."[43]

The *Commercial Bulletin*, a new newspaper in St. Louis, commented on this incident, viewing it as a terrible thing. No man should send antislavery literature "in the same parcel with the sacred volume! Is this his religion? Is this his 'good will to all men'?" The editorial added ominously that Lovejoy was being "watched," that his "slightest movement" would bring punishment, and that he would be "put down."[44] Lovejoy called the editor "well-meaning but weak-minded." Friends told Lovejoy that if he had been in Jefferson City when the Bibles arrived, he would have been the victim of a mob. Lovejoy responded in his newspaper: "I am not aware that any law of my country forbids my sending what document I please to a friend or citizen. I know, indeed, that mob-law has decided otherwise. . . . I have never knowingly sent any abolition publication to a single individual in Missouri or elsewhere; I claim the right to send ten thousand of them if I choose. Whether I will exercise that right or not, is for me, and not for the mob, to decide." He then quoted the Missouri state constitution: "Every person may freely speak, write, and print on any subject." He added: "The truth is, my fellow citizens, if you give ground a single inch, there is no stopping place. I deem it, therefore, my duty to take my stand upon the Constitution."[45]

Lovejoy's mother heard about the St. Louis situation, and to reduce her concerns, Lovejoy wrote: "We are getting quiet again. The Lynchites are getting ashamed of their doings. The Papists, the Irish, and the pro-slavery Christians, finding that I am not to be driven nor frightened away, are beginning to feel and act a little more reasonably. A large majority of the Protestants in the city are decidedly with me."[46] In an appeal for funds to a wealthy New York opponent of slavery, Lovejoy wrote: "There was a time when I did not know but I should become the victim of popular vengeance, but I do not now think there is so much danger."[47] To add to Lovejoy's optimism, the *Missouri Republican* commented: "When Mr. Lovejoy . . . undertakes to say that the citizens of St. Louis, or any respectable portion of them, ever expressed an intention of mobbing him, or destroy[ing] the office of the 'Observer', we feel called upon to say that he does great injustice to our city. . . . A mob cannot be got up in St. Louis to do an unlawful act."[48] Even though the editorial had an anti-Lovejoy tone, it appealed to the better nature of Missouri citizens, but that optimistic view of the situation did not last long.

Five slaves escaped into Illinois, and a posse of sixty men formed to get them. The posse crossed into neighboring Illinois, where they assumed the slaves had fled. Illinois was a free state in theory but with strong Southern ties and sympathies, and Illinoisans had no objection to Missouri residents crossing the border to recover their "property" that had escaped. Runaway slaves were not too difficult to find since they had dark skin among a population almost entirely white-skinned. In addition, their "Negro clothes," clothing ordinarily worn by slaves, distinguished them from the few free former slaves in Illinois.

The posse of sixty men found the slaves and two white men who, someone charged, had helped the slaves escape. The slaves and the two whites were brought back to St. Louis. The posse quickly built a hanging structure in a wooded spot near St. Louis and at first threatened the two white men with immediate death. The posse hesitated, however, because neither man confessed to any guilt and because some Methodists in the group did not believe in execution. Someone shouted that the two white men should be whipped first and then hung after they had confessed. The group divided again on this point. Finally, they decided that each of the approximately sixty men present would give the two white men five lashes with the whip. The two were told they would be whipped until they confessed. After one victim had received approximately 150 lashes, he cried out professing his guilt. The other man, after 50 additional lashes, still professed innocence. The second man clearly would die before admitting guilt. They were both then locked in jail. No one ever produced evidence that either was guilty, and eventually they were released, but this incident—plus riots and mob scenes around the nation—aroused people, and in St. Louis, Lovejoy became the center of the tension.

At the end of September 1835, Lovejoy left to go to Union, Missouri, for an area Presbyterian meeting, followed by a statewide meeting at Marion, Missouri. At Union, he introduced some antislavery resolutions that were adopted unanimously. At Marion, he ran into difficulty, for a church official coming directly from St. Louis reported "a thousand frightful things" about the happenings in St. Louis. People there were exceedingly angry, and destructive action seemed almost inevitable, he told them. He said that Presbyterianism would disappear in Missouri if they maintained an antislavery stance. Other reports from St. Louis were similar. The antislavery resolution did not pass at the Marion meeting. A majority of ministers voted for it, but the lay members defeated it. Lovejoy commented in a letter: "Two ministers from New England voted against us, a fact as lamentable as it is true. Eastern men, when they go over, constitute the most ultra defenders of slavery."[49] Fears grew for Lovejoy's life.

Celia Ann Lovejoy was in St. Charles, Missouri, because the couple expected their first child, and she was experiencing a difficult pregnancy. "The brethren told me I had no right to sacrifice her, whatever I might do with myself," Lovejoy wrote his brother Joseph. When he got to St. Charles, he found his wife still sick, and for three days Lovejoy, too, was ill. "By this time I had fully made up my mind that duty to my Lord and Master required my presence at St. Louis. My friends advised me not to go; all but my wife. She said, 'Go if you think duty calls you.'

Accordingly I came into St. Louis." He temporarily left Celia Ann in St. Charles. When he arrived in St. Louis, he "found the community in a state of dreadful alarm and excitement. The press were fanning the flames. . . . On my arrival, men came to me and told me I could not walk the streets of St. Louis by night or by day."[50]

During Lovejoy's absence from St. Louis, a number of things had happened to cause even greater excitement. The first issue of the *Observer* that appeared while Lovejoy traveled to the Presbyterian Synod had this notice: "Since the Editor left, the Publishers of the *Observer* have received a communication from the owners of this paper, advising an entire suspension of all controversy upon the exciting subject of slavery. As this course is entirely agreeable to the feelings and views of the publishers, nothing upon the subject will appear in its columns during the absence of the Editor. Upon his return the communication will be submitted to him, and the future course of the paper finally arranged."[51]

Two issues later, Lovejoy had not yet returned, but the intensity of feeling against Lovejoy and the *Observer* mounted. The owners urged calm: "We believe this to be a momentary excitement arising out of the apprehension of the white men who stole Major Dougherty's negroes, and who having been dealt with according to the new code by several of our most respectable citizens, and that they will see to it that no evil arises out of that excitement."[52]

A meeting of owners to discuss Lovejoy's situation — and theirs — and to urge that he avoid the slavery issue included many of his friends. Some were frightened for Lovejoy, some for themselves. The greatest disappointment to Lovejoy was that Rev. William Potts, the minister of the First Presbyterian Church, attended the meeting. Potts had persuaded Lovejoy to enter the ministry and had married Celia and Elijah, but he was also one of the owners of the *Observer*. When Lovejoy refused to change his position, the owners demanded that he resign as editor. Lovejoy had no choice. He thought he had lost the fight. The owners then turned the property over to the man who held the mortgage. That man had no use for printing equipment without an editor, and he surprised everyone, including Lovejoy, by asking the controversial editor to stay on.

During Lovejoy's absence, there had been more and more talk about mob action against him. One group actually formed, preparing to attack the *Observer* office, but when the owners threatened gunfire on anyone attacking the plant, they changed their minds. One of the local newspapers, in commenting on Lovejoy, noted ominously that the church would soon be free of its rotten sheep. If people expected all this to frighten Lovejoy from his stand, they were badly mistaken. He stood firm, even stronger than before, despite the fact that he was now a father as well as a husband. In March 1835, one year after their marriage, Celia Ann gave birth to a son, whom the Lovejoys named Edward Payson, after a Congregational minister. His son then had the same initials: E. P. Lovejoy.

Lovejoy's firm stand made the supporters of slavery even more furious. An assembly of citizens, including future U.S. Senator Thomas Hart Benton, passed a resolution to stop all antislavery talk, specifically that of Lovejoy and his newspaper. The resolution of the meeting called Lovejoy and his friends "misguided fanatics." It also pointed out that freedom of speech does not give the right "to freely discuss the question of slavery, either orally or through the medium of the press." Slavery, the resolution said, was "too nearly allied to the vital interests of the slaveholding States" to be publicly discussed. It also raised the explosive issue of racially mixed marriages, calling "the doctrine of amalgamation . . . peculiarly baneful to the interests and happiness of society. The union of black and white . . . we consider the most preposterous and impudent doctrine advanced by the Abolitionist, as repugnant to judgment and science as it is degrading to the feelings of all sensitive minds." The group also dealt with Lovejoy's religious basis for opposing slavery, noting "that the sacred writings furnish abundant evidence of the existence of Slavery from the earliest periods. The Patriarchs and Prophets possessed slaves—our Saviour recognised the relation between master and slave, and deprecated it not. . . . We consider Slavery as it now exists in the United States, as sanctioned by the sacred Scriptures."[53] Those at the meeting called for the appointment of a "Committee of Vigilance" to see that their wishes were carried out in case city officials failed to act. The Committee of Vigilance would consist of seven people from each ward, twenty for the St. Louis suburbs and seven for each township in St. Louis County. They clearly called for action, legal or illegal.

Lovejoy responded with fighting words, admitting that he wrote and published them at the peril of his life. Lovejoy noted that the Committee of Vigilance consisted "of seven for each ward, twenty for the suburbs, and seven for each township in the county—in all EIGHTY THREE persons whose duty it shall be to report to the Mayor or other civil authorities, all persons *suspected* of preaching abolition doctrines, &c., and should the civil authorities fail to deal with them, on *suspicion*, why then the Committee are to call a meeting of the citizens and execute their decrees—in other words, to *lynch* the suspected persons" (Lovejoy's italics). Lovejoy said he would not give in, either to the owners who wanted to muzzle him or to the people who wanted to silence him. He wrote: "I am threatened with violence and death because I dare to advocate, in any way, the cause of the oppressed. Under a deep sense of my obligations to my country, the church and my God, I declare it to be my fixed purpose to submit to no such dictation. And I am prepared to abide the consequences."[54]

Lovejoy became vehement in denouncing his opponents' religious defense of slavery: "I have not words to express my utter abhorrence of such a sentiment. My soul detests it, my heart sickens over it; my judgment, my understanding, my conscience, reject it, with loathing and horror. What is the system of Slavery 'as it now exists in the United States?' It is a system of buying and selling immortal beings for the sake of gain; a system which forbids to man and woman the rights of husband and wife, sanctioning the dissolution of this tie at the mere caprice of another; a system which tolerates the existence of a class of men whose professed business it is to go about from house to house, tearing husband and wife, parent and child asunder, chaining their victims together, and then driving them with a whip, like so many mules, to a distant market, there to be disposed of to the highest bidder." He asked, "Is this the land of Freedom or Despotism?" He added words that he would repeat in Alton soon, words for which he would be remembered: "I can die at my post, but I cannot desert it."[55]

Lovejoy urged citizens not to damage the *Observer* office, explaining that the office belongs "to the young men who print the paper; and they are in no way responsible for the matter appearing in its columns. If the popular vengeance needs a victim, I offer myself a willing sacrifice." In his defense, Lovejoy asked, "Why is it that this storm of persecution is directed against me? What have I done? Have I libelled any man's person or character? No. Have I been found in gambling-houses, billiard-rooms, or tippling-shops? Never. Have I ever disturbed the peace and quiet of your city by midnight revellings, or riots in the streets? It is not pretended." And he warned: "As Phalaris was the first man roasted in the brazen ball he had constructed for the tyrant of Sicily, so the inventor of the guillotine was by no means the last, whose neck had practical experience of the keenness of its edge." Lovejoy said he faced death with no misgiving, but for "one string tugging at my heart": the concern for his wife. He wrote that he confronted such violence "freely forgiving my enemies, even those who thirst for my blood."[56]

But in his editorials, Lovejoy did not merely express a passive willingness to accept the consequences of what he had written. He vigorously restated his earlier stands and went beyond them. He attacked the most sensitive problem of all. His accusers called him an amalgamationist, a term used to describe those who believed in the intermarriage of the two races. Lovejoy denied that he favored interracial marriage, but he hinted publicly at what newspapers never printed—the common sexual abuse of enslaved women by white owners. The worst treatment of the Negro is not the public whipping, he wrote, but what takes place "in their cabins." Everyone knew what he meant. He was not an amalgamationist, but he noted that there are some "practical amalgamationists." Then he added: "Unless my eyes deceive me as I walk the streets of our city, there are some among us who venture to put it into practice."[57] No one had ever talked like that in print in St. Louis.

In the November 19, 1835, edition, Lovejoy wrote: "The number of today closes the second year of the paper. Through good and through evil report, we have struggled on thus far amidst many difficulties. . . . Dear brethren, the responsibility now rests with you. Shall the Observer be sustained? Shall the press dare to speak out freely, or shall it be muzzled? We make it our request that all who feel an interest in this subject, in any way, would communicate with the Editor. . . . We ask that those who approve, as well as those who disapprove our course, would inform us of their sentiments." Perhaps in part to bolster his own spirits, as well as to let the community know of support for him, a few weeks later Lovejoy printed a series of letters from people — primarily living outside of Missouri—encouraging him and praising him for his courageous stands.

The tension of November 1835 carried into December, when someone printed a handbill calling for a mass meeting to "put down the vile slander of E. P. Lovejoy." Six weeks after the initial citizens' meeting, "an adjourned meeting" of the group met and again called upon Lovejoy to stop all discussion on slavery, which "has been calculated to injure the peace and wellbeing of this community—to endanger the lives and property of our fellow-citizens." The final portion of the resolution read: "In the opinion of the Meeting there ought to be no school of literacy instruction for negroes and mulattoes."[58]

Three days before writing his stinging, strong response to the first resolution and meeting, he wrote one of his brothers: "I am here . . . at the daily peril of my life."[59]

ᚢ A Horrible Murder

Lovejoy lived from day to day never knowing whether he would see another sunset. He wrote his mother: "We have a man here, walking our streets in open day, who, about a year since, actually whipped his negro woman to death. He was tried for the murder, but as negro evidence was not admitted, he could not be convicted, or rather was not. Such men are not mobbed, but he who ventures to say that Slavery is a sin, does it at the risk of his life."[1]

Another St. Louis newspaper now forcefully entered the picture. The *Missouri Republican* said that meetings like the anti-Lovejoy sessions "are productive of much more harm than good," and the newspaper called on citizens not to unite "in a crusade against the liberty of the press."[2] This was the first time so powerful a force had stood up—not in agreement with Lovejoy, but in defense of his right to express whatever opinions he had. That, plus the cooling effects of winter, calmed things somewhat for a short while.

During this period, Lovejoy made a trip to Alton because he was considering a move to the free state of Illinois. Alton area civic and religious leaders were enthusiastic about the idea, but Lovejoy decided to stay in St. Louis. He felt that some might regard his moving away as a flight from danger. Besides, the worst period of tension appeared to be past. He did keep Alton in the back of his mind, however. A few months later, he wrote a few lines about what a fine place Alton was and about the spirit of liberality there.

In addition to his other troubles, Lovejoy still had financial problems. The Illinois Synod of the Presbyterian Church heard about his strong antislavery stand and by resolution withdrew its support of the *Observer*. Six ministers at the meeting strongly protested such action, and perhaps as a compromise, the Synod passed an antislavery resolution, but the withdrawal of support for the *Observer* stood.[3] Lovejoy editorialized that he had financial troubles and that subscribers would have to pay their subscriptions for the *Observer* to continue to "dare to speak out freely." In a letter, he said the *Observer* could continue only "if the Christian public will support it."[4]

Nevertheless, in addition to his physical and financial threats, Lovejoy also received encouragement. Rev. Edward Beecher, president of the new college at Jacksonville, Illinois (and brother of the future author of *Uncle Tom's Cabin*), wrote, enclosing twenty dollars and stating that between one hundred and two hundred dollars more would be raised for the paper. Beecher said that Lovejoy had spoken "with the courage demanded in a soldier of the cross" and that "the time for silence has gone by."[5]

On New Year's Eve, 1835, the *Observer* noted "the baptism of an infant slave. It was the first case of the kind we ever witnessed."[6] There continued to be letters to the newspaper and editorial comments on slavery, including the blunt declaration that slavery is a sin, but life gradually became more peaceful. This did not mean that people in St. Louis liked Lovejoy or what he said, but there seemed to be little they could do about it. In March 1836, the *Alton Telegraph* published a speech by a North Carolina judge on the "evils of mobocracy," adding: "Men who unchain a mob are like men who unchain the plague and pestilence—it may rid them . . . of their enemies but will also sweep them away in its poisonous career."[7]

Less than a month later, the issue of mob rule suddenly exploded, caused by the murder of one man and the burning alive of another. Witnesses and newspaper accounts differ somewhat on minor details, but what follows is the sad, gruesome story.[8] Francis McIntosh of Pittsburgh, Pennsylvania, a free African American described by Lovejoy as "a mulatto fellow,"[9] worked as a porter and cook on the steamboat *Flora*, which docked in St. Louis on Thursday afternoon, April 28, 1836. The *Lady Jackson* also docked there. Both boats had been in Louisville. McIntosh, whom a fellow crew member described as quiet and good-natured, had met in Louisville a free African American young woman, a chambermaid on the *Lady Jackson*, and had fallen in love with her. The *Lady Jackson* got to St. Louis a few hours ahead of the boat on which McIntosh worked. When the *Flora* arrived and McIntosh had finished his work, he put on a bright red jacket given him by a New Orleans gambler and walked off the boat, intending to visit his friend on the *Lady Jackson*.

Exactly what happened next is not clear. The captain of the *Flora* said that two officers—George Hammond, deputy sheriff, and William Mull, deputy constable, neither of whom was in uniform—were chasing a sailor who had been fighting and shouted at McIntosh to stop the pursued man when he went past. McIntosh did nothing, and the officers arrested him. Perhaps the two who had been fighting were from McIntosh's boat or perhaps McIntosh did not know that the two men who asked for his help were officers. Perhaps McIntosh was simply afraid to become involved. The other version of the arrest is that two members of the *Flora* crew had been drinking and had gotten into trouble with the officers. McIntosh tried to help them and was arrested.

After he was taken before the justice of the peace and charged with breach of the peace, McIntosh was ordered to jail. For a free African American, to be arrested in a slave state was a frightening prospect, for it might mean a return to slavery. When McIntosh asked Hammond and Mull how long he would have to be in jail, they told him at least five years. He had no attorney, and he knew that as an African American, he would get none in Missouri. McIntosh then suddenly turned on the two officers, pulled a knife, and lunged first at Mull. He missed him but quickly lunged again, catching Mull on the right side of his chest, seriously wounding him. Crazed with fear, McIntosh then turned on Hammond, who held his shoulder. He struck the lower part of Hammond's chin and neck, cutting the jugular vein. Hammond started to flee, walked about sixty- feet bleeding profusely, and dropped dead.

The small crowd that had gathered to watch McIntosh being taken to jail were stunned into inaction during the deadly fight that took only seconds. After wounding Hammond, McIntosh started to run. Despite his serious wound, Mull joined others in following McIntosh, shouting for his capture. His shouts aroused people in the neighborhood, who joined in the pursuit of McIntosh. They quickly caught the frightened man and placed him in jail.

In the meantime, someone told Hammond's widow about her husband's death, and she and her children came and found him dead on the street in a pool of blood, surrounded by a group of curious and sympathetic townspeople. Mrs. Hammond had some type of obvious physical handicap — what, we do not know. One newspaper referred to her simply as "afflicted."[10] People saw this moving scene of a physically disabled woman, suddenly a widow, and her children screaming and crying beside the body of the well-liked Hammond. (Lovejoy described him as "an intelligent, upright man, and an excellent officer.")[11] The scene so moved many of those gathered that they wanted to see "justice" done immediately. It seemed only minutes after the slaying took place that people started collecting, and the demand grew for immediate vengeance. Soon the crowd became a mob, moved to the jail, and asked for McIntosh. The sheriff at first tried to resist, but his family occupied a part of the jail as living quarters, and he feared for their safety. Rather than turn McIntosh over to the crowd, which he knew would violate his sworn duty, he took his family and escaped, leaving McIntosh locked in the jail but taking the keys with him.

The mob continued to demand McIntosh's life, and the absence of the sheriff increased their determination. One man— not identified in any newspaper— stood up and tried to halt them. He said that the courts would handle the matter quickly, but that was not quick enough for the growing number of people, then about five hundred, and the man saw that he would lose his life if he continued his opposition. Tools were then brought to break down the jail door. While men worked at getting the doors down, an intense quiet settled over the growing crowd. People spoke in whispers. Others were armed and stood by to make sure no one would stop them.

It took more than an hour for the mob to get through the jail door to McIntosh's cell. When they reached the prisoner, there was a shout of triumph from a crowd that wanted blood. They dragged McIntosh out of the jail. Some grabbed him by the legs, some by the arms, and one grabbed his hair. They carried him to the edge of town not far from the jail. The mob now numbered more than two thousand. The *Missouri Republican* said "several thousand persons witnessed the revolting spectacle," and the *Missouri Argus* referred to "the gathering thousands."[12] One witness recalled, probably with exaggeration, that there were "5,000 howling, crazy people."[13]

They chained McIntosh to a large locust tree, his back against the trunk of the tree, facing south and facing the people who brought him there. They piled wood around him, mainly rail ties and old planks, as high as his knees. Shavings were brought, and someone got a hot brand—the kind used on horses and livestock. They touched the brand to the shavings and started a fire. Up to this point, McIntosh had said nothing. When the fire started, he begged for someone in the crowd to shoot him, but no one moved to offer him help. One report has it that a lawyer named Riddle wanted the crowd to see what a terrible thing they had done and for that reason helped to prevent people from shooting him. The story seems doubtful, and the other accounts contain no such incident.

In any event, when McIntosh pleaded for someone to shoot him, no one did. From that point on, he sang hymns and prayed while the crowd watched. After a few minutes, his features became disfigured by the flames, and he became silent. Someone said that he apparently was out of his misery, and McIntosh replied distinctly: "No, no. I feel as much as any of you. I hear you all. Shoot me! Shoot me!"[14] Between ten and twenty minutes after the fire started, McIntosh died.

An old African American named Louis was given seventy-five cents for keeping the fire burning during the night. The crowd, apparently quiet and orderly after his death, disappeared quickly, a few to taverns but most to their homes. The next morning, a black and disfigured corpse could be seen. A group of boys started throwing stones at the remains, the object of their game being to see who could first succeed in breaking the skull.

Deeply moved and depressed by all of this, though he was out of the city during the hours it occurred, Lovejoy began his editorial in the next *Observer*: "Our hand trembles as we record the story." Near the editorial's conclusion, he wrote: "We visited the scene of the burning on the day following, about noon. We stood and gazed for a moment or two, upon the blackened and mutilated trunk—for that was all which remained—of McIntosh before us, and as we turned away, in bitterness of heart we prayed that we might not live."[15] A week later, what had happened still so moved Lovejoy that he wrote that he continued to pray for death.

While Lovejoy talked more plainly than did the *Missouri Republican*, it also found the mob action "revolting."[16] Across the Mississippi River, the newly established *Alton Telegraph* likewise condemned the mob. In Springfield, Illinois, a young state legislator named Abraham Lincoln gave a talk before the Young Men's Lyceum, warning against "the growing disposition to substitute the wild and furious passions" for the law. No other legislator in either Illinois or Missouri condemned the crowd action. Lincoln talked about "worse than savage mobs" at "that horror-striking scene in St. Louis."[17]

From across the river at Alton, Elijah's brother, John Lovejoy, wrote to their mother: "One of the most horrid, barbarous, brutal, inhuman and outrageous deeds that ever occurred in this country took place Thursday night last at St. Louis. . . . Now they say that they will burn every boat that brings a negro into port [in St. Louis]."[18]

In the Illinois capital city of Vandalia, the *Illinois State Register* commented: "What is our country coming to? . . . Are the laws to be put down, and Lynch law to become the order of the day?"[19] But in its next issue, the newspaper made clear it opposed Abolition: "The whole number of signers to the Abolition memorials presented to Congress during this session is said to be only twenty-seven thousand. Ten thousand of whom are women and three thousand minors; leaving fourteen thousand men in the United States for Abolition."[20]

The next week, the *Missouri Republican* noted that some Eastern Abolitionists were trying to gather together the bones of McIntosh "with the intention of forwarding them to the Atlantic States. The use to be made of them there, must be obvious." The *Missouri Republican* warned the people of the Eastern states to be "upon their guard" against this "dastardly means" of promoting the antislavery cause.[21]

Reinforcing such fears, one of the publications most hated by slavery supporters, the *Emancipator* of New York City, roared editorially: "The circumstances attending the burning of a negro alive, at the West, are known. Much is said of Santa Anna's

cruelty—much of the bloodthirstiness of the Russian emper-
or. . . . Well does the *Atlas* say: 'The Spaniards may have
murdered monks by the score; the Mexicans may have shot
prisoners by the dozen; but roasting alive before a slow fire is a
practice nowhere except among free, enlightened, high-minded
Americans.' "[22]

Elijah Lovejoy spared no editorial words in condemning the
McIntosh slaying. He called the whispering at the scene whispers "which made the blood curdle to hear," and he described the
action as "savage barbarity." He furthermore called upon all
who participated—which must have been the majority of citizens—to "seek forgiveness." No one could have spoken more
strongly or with more courage against the "spirit of mobism."
Lovejoy wrote: "In Charlestown it burns a Convent over the head
of defenseless women . . . in Vicksburg it hangs up gamblers,
three or four in a row; and in St. Louis it forces a man . . . to the
stake and burns him alive!"[23]

The public greeted the strong Lovejoy stand in the *Observer*
with extreme disfavor. There were renewed threats of violence
and also minor damage to the *Observer* office. One night someone stole the composing sticks used to hold hand-set type,
equipment vital to produce a newspaper in 1836 before the
inception of automatic typesetting equipment. The next noon
when everyone went out to lunch, one or more people stole more
equipment. The *Observer* commented: "Any information which
may lead to the detection of those engaged in this mean business
will be gratefully received."[24] A week later, someone destroyed
the completed type for printing the newspaper. The next edition
of the *Observer* came out in dramatically reduced form, but
Lovejoy told his readers: "As soon as the necessary material can
be obtained and put together, the larger size will appear."[25]

Some of this violence to the *Observer* happened while Lovejoy, with his wife, attended the national meeting of the Presby-

terian Church in Pittsburgh as the official delegate for the Presbyterians in the St. Louis area. While there, he became part of a minority that suffered defeat, 154–87, in an attempt to get the Presbyterian Church nationally to take a strong stand against slavery. The motion prevailed to postpone indefinitely any action on the issue. Lovejoy and twenty-six others then filed a protest that was entered into the proceedings. When the convention ended, he and his wife headed back to St. Louis. They stopped four days in Peoria and confided to some friends that they were thinking of moving their operation to Alton. When they returned home, Lovejoy noted in an editorial: "After an absence lengthened considerably beyond his expectations the Editor has returned to his duties. He comes back with health even better than when he left, and, as he trusts, with renewed purpose to spend and be spent in the service of his Divine Master."[26]

Before the Lovejoys arrived in St. Louis, they heard about the damage that had been done to the *Observer* equipment. This came as no great surprise, but the conduct of the judge who handled the investigation of the mob slaying of McIntosh amazed them. The judge could not have been better named by Gilbert and Sullivan: Luke Edward Lawless. A man of controversy in the community, he had once served time in jail for contempt of court. A fifty-three-year-old slave owner, Judge Lawless was satisfied with the community's culture—slavery and all. Fifteen months earlier when Lawless had been named to the bench, the *Missouri Republican* noted that he was appointed by the governor *"during good behavior"* (italics in original).[27] Nine months later, the same newspaper observed: "We neither acknowledge his wisdom, respect his character, believe in his honesty or purpose, or his freedom from prejudice. We think him a most unfit man in every respect for the station in which accident has placed him."[28]

When the McIntosh slaying came before his court, Judge

Lawless told the grand jury that what happened to Francis McIntosh violated the law and was a tragedy. From there, Judge Lawless proceeded to make one of the most amazing speeches to the grand jury in the history of our nation's courts. First, he essentially told the grand jury not to find anyone guilty of the McIntosh slaying, and then he proceeded to blame Lovejoy for what had happened! As Judge Lawless said to the grand jury: "If the destruction of the murderer of Hammond was the act of congregated thousands, seized by an almost electric frenzy, which, in all ages and nations, has hurried on the infuriated multitude to deeds of death and destruction, then, I say, act not at all in the matter; the case is beyond the reach of human law."[29] In the course of his remarks to the grand jury, Judge Lawless also said that he had saved Lovejoy and the *Observer* office from the destruction that would have come from Lovejoy's remarks over the McIntosh slaying. ("We do not believe him," Lovejoy wrote.)[30]

Judge Lawless then went on to condemn Lovejoy and the *Observer* instead of the mob and its leaders. Newspapers like the *Observer* "fanaticize the negro and excite him against the white man," Judge Lawless told the grand jury. The judge then cited several quotations from the *Observer*, such as: "Slavery is a sin and ought to be abandoned." Judge Lawless told the jurors: "It seems to me impossible, that while such language is used and published as that which I have cited from the St. Louis *Observer*, there can be safety in a slaveholding state." The judge noted the last sentence of a letter to the editor that read: "Heaven grant I may never be the master of a slave."[31] Judge Lawless said that this type of language urged slaves to revolt.

Then Judge Lawless asked for action against Lovejoy. "It is all important," he said, "that the negro population within our bounds should be saved from the corrupting influence to which I have thought it my duty to call your attention. . . . But it will be asked, is there no remedy for this monstrous evil? I am compelled to answer that I know of none. No law exists, that I know of, to punish this crime against the peace and rights of the people of Missouri." He asked the grand jury to consider what could be done. The judge said he favored freedom of the press, but he could "see no reason why the Press should be a means of widespread mischief. . . . Are we to be the victims of those sanctimonious madmen?" He added that he hoped the next session of the legislature would adopt measures "to punish, if they cannot prevent, those exhortations to rebellion."[32] The grand jury did what the judge had told them to do: they found no one guilty.

Reaction to Judge Lawless's speech came rapidly. The *New York American* said it read the speech with "surprise and disgust." It also noted the odd coincidence of his name, Lawless. The Pittsburgh *Christian Herald* called the judge's statement "an outrage on all law, morality, and decency." The Jacksonville (Ill.) *Patriot* noted that the judge's ideas strike at "the very root of our liberties."[33] The *Emancipator* examined Judge Lawless's thesis that if a few commit a crime, they can be found guilty, but if many are involved, they cannot. The newspaper suggested that "if this doctrine is good for the criminal, why not for the judge. . . . Why should not the 'many' take the judge in hand, and 'duck' or 'slick' or 'lynch' him? Plainly they should."[34]

Lovejoy responded as his readers would have expected. He would rather "be chained to the same tree as McIntosh and share his fate" than to accept the ideas of Judge Lawless. Lovejoy said that the answer is to enforce the laws. Until then, mobs will continue to "destroy, plunder and burn." The fiery editorial added: "We covet not the loss of property, nor the honors of martyrdom; but better, far better, that the office of the *Observer* should be scattered in fragments to the four winds than that the doctrines promoted by Judge Lawless from the bench should be

adopted in this community."[35] Lovejoy also charged the judge
with encouraging future mobs to take illegal action.

Between irritating the McIntosh observers and participants —
who possibly constituted a majority of St. Louis's citizens — and
liquor dispensers and various religious groups, Lovejoy had
angered almost every powerful group and person in the city. In
writing his editorial, Lovejoy not only attacked what the judge
said, but bending to one of his weaknesses, he also attacked
Judge Lawless because of his Roman Catholic affiliation, calling
the Irish-born Lawless "a foreigner" and "a papist." But Roman
Catholics were not the only people he attacked. A few weeks
earlier, Lovejoy had made some less than laudatory comments
about a Presbyterian minister, Rev. H. Chamberlain, that
prompted the pastor to put an item in another local paper: "TO
THE PUBLIC. The last Saint Louis *Observer* contains an assault
on my character, injurious to me as a man, as a citizen of this
community, and a minister of the gospel of Christ."[36]

Lovejoy grew up in a home with strong religious convictions — and prejudices. In probably the last letter the Lovejoy
brothers received from their mother before Elijah's death, Elizabeth Lovejoy included a three-page religious discourse in
which she denounced "papists" and added: "Pray for the conversion of the poor ignorant Catholics. The priests make them
believe they are doing good service when they are killing the
wicked heretics."[37] Lovejoy's childhood home accepted malicious rumors and unfounded superstition about Roman Catholics, and unfortunately, that upbringing shaped his attitudes. He
attacked Catholics for, among other things, their use of candles
and vestments. At one point, he editorialized: "The real origin
of the cry 'Down with the *Observer*' is . . . Popery. The fire that
is now blazing and crackling through this city, was kindled on
Papish altars and has been assiduously blowed up by Jesuit
breath."[38] The Roman Catholic newspaper for the St. Louis

diocese, *Shepherd of the Valley*, responded in terms that were generally milder than Lovejoy's attacks, though at one point, it referred to him as a "forger and slanderer."[39] Another issue described Lovejoy as "a weak, unprincipled man, whose endeavors are calculated to create anything but brotherly love between Catholics and Protestants, but it is not true that any Catholic in this community . . . bears any hatred towards [him]; and we are certain that the clergy harbor nothing but pity for him."[40]

Unfortunately, the Lovejoy household was not alone in its strong anti-Catholic bias. Anti-Catholic sentiment dominated the attitudes and actions of most of the colonies before an independent United States emerged, and such sentiment held sway over much of the nation well into this century, dominating presidential elections. It gradually declined until the unusual combination of the elections of John F. Kennedy to the presidency and John XXIII as Pope brought about a dramatic improvement in attitudes. Before the publication of *Uncle Tom's Cabin*, perhaps the most widely circulated book in the United States was a fraudulent book alleging all types of abuses taking place in a Montreal convent. After Lincoln's assassination, his Secretary of War, Edwin Stanton, believed Lincoln's death was a Roman Catholic plot.[41]

Lovejoy's bigoted remarks against Catholics do not excuse Judge Lawless's outrageous request for action against Lovejoy or his assurance that the illegal action of a crowd would not result in court action against either them or their leaders. Another item of information indicated to potential evildoers that they should act quickly against Lovejoy. The same issue of the *Observer* that denounced Judge Lawless contained an announcement that Lovejoy would be moving his newspaper operations to Alton.

For fear of violent action, particularly against his wife and newborn son, Lovejoy finally decided to move his newspaper across the river. He could operate on free territory, he thought, without losing any of his subscribers or his influence. Because of constant threats and his wife's poor health, Lovejoy had earlier moved his wife and son to her home in St. Charles. He wanted to face the possibly violent response in St. Louis alone. Now he felt they should move to Alton where they could live together without fear. His announcement stated: "After much delibera- tion, and consultation with a number of our friends, we have determined hereafter to issue the *Observer* from Alton." He hoped to keep all of his subscribers in St. Louis, and he felt the paper would be "better supported there than it is now."[42]

The conflict in which Lovejoy was involved gave his news- paper national importance. Subscription lists grew, and a few weeks after the McIntosh slaying, the *Observer* announced that it would now be one-third larger. Lovejoy had no intention of losing his growing national influence. Perhaps another factor in his decision to move to Alton was that in northern Missouri people had driven his friend Rev. David Nelson out of the state. The minister whom Lovejoy credited for his conversion to Christianity made no apologies for his strong antislavery stand, and he spoke with conviction and power. He would not adminis- ter the religious rite of communion to anyone who owned slaves. When Rev. Nelson read from the pulpit an appeal for contribu- tions to settle freed slaves in Africa, it caused an immediate uproar. A fight broke out in the church, and one man was stabbed. These incidents seemed to be too much for residents of a slave state, and they forced Rev. Nelson to leave.

About eleven o'clock the evening after the *Observer*'s blister- ing editorial and announcement appeared, a group of men started roaming the streets of St. Louis. They carried a drum with them and marched from street to street beating the drum, asking for volunteers to destroy the *Observer*'s plant. By midnight, they had gathered approximately two hundred men and headed for the

Observer. In a short time, they had broken the doors and began destroying equipment and scattering type. Lovejoy's brother John, who was living with him at the time, had a trunk full of clothing in the office. The mob carried it to the river and threw it in, including four dollars John had hidden in the trunk. They also pushed printing equipment into the Mississippi. Some of it they broke and left in the print shop. Not stopping there, they threw into the river the furniture that Lovejoy and his wife had bought from careful savings, as well as some gifts the Lovejoys had received after their marriage. The total damage was at least seven hundred dollars, according to Lovejoy, a significant sum in 1836.

One of the aldermen, Bryan Mullanphy, a leader among Roman Catholics in St. Louis and secretary of the Western Catholic Association, tried to stop the men — at the hazard of his life, Lovejoy wrote — but with no success. He had no police backing and could gather no immediate support from other city officials. The *Missouri Republican* found the mob action "dreadful" and took a clear stand for obedience to the law: "We put aside altogether the individual whose conduct has furnished a pretended excuse for this outrageous violation of the law. His publication may have been imprudent; but that he had a right — a constitutional right — is a position which we hold. . . . Where is this thing to end? . . . Who can feel himself secure when 15 or 20 men are permitted, for hours, to perambulate the city, beating [a drum] for recruits, and then, without molestation, to break into houses and cast all they contain to the winds? Protect the property of every citizen, no matter how obnoxious he may be to any portion of the community."[43] The *Missouri Arms*, also published in St. Louis, totally ignored the destruction of Lovejoy's equipment. The mayor of St. Louis quickly called for the trial of some of the rioters, but the court found no one guilty.

John Lovejoy wrote his mother: "I suppose Parish [the family's name for Elijah] has written to you the particulars of the recent transactions in St. Louis. . . . They are outrageous, uncivilized, fiendish, and dangerous to the preservation of our government. . . . The doctrine of Abolitionism I hate, but am almost determined to be one. . . . The opponents of the doctrine are making themselves so perfectly ridiculous that it is causing to disgust every person who has the remotest feeling of honor or justice or, in fact, of good breeding. . . . On account of this and their ruthless course in destroying [a] person's property, were I able, I would instantly leave the country and go back to the 'land of steady habits.' . . . Tell all the people in that section of the country who are doing a good business, not to leave it and come here. Their property is not safe; their lives are not safe; and, in fact, nothing is safe. Stay where you are, and live peaceably and happily." He added: "Parish is well and in fine spirits. Not the least depressed."[44]

Celia Ann Lovejoy — temporarily in St. Charles — stood up well under all this. She was a strong, vibrant woman when she and Elijah married. He wrote to his mother: "My dear wife is a perfect heroine. Though of delicate health, she endures affliction more calmly than I had supposed possible for a woman to do. Never has she, by a single word, attempted to turn me from the scene of warfare and danger; never has she whispered a feeling of discontent at the hardships to which she has been subjected in consequence of her marriage to me. She has seen me shunned, hated, and reviled, by those who were once my dearest friends. She has heard them curse and threaten me, and she has only clung to me the more closely and more devotedly. When I told her that the mob had destroyed a considerable portion of our furniture, she said: 'It does not matter what they have destroyed since they have not hurt you.' Such is woman! And such is the woman God has given me."[45]

Many St. Louis friends now urged Lovejoy to stay in St. Louis and fight it out, arguing that to go to Alton would mean surrendering to the mob, but Lovejoy decided to proceed to move to Alton. His big printing press itself was not ruined, although the ruffians had turned over the large, heavy piece of equipment. Lovejoy arranged to send the press to Alton, together with smaller items of printing equipment that he had salvaged.

Alton, with a population of more than twenty-five hundred, seemed destined to surpass St. Louis in population to become the largest city in its own state of Illinois. A former mayor of both Alton and St. Louis wrote of this period: "In the East, [Alton] was even more talked of than St. Louis, as the coming Western city."[46] An election in Illinois to determine the capital city ended with Alton as the choice, even though the state legislature did not follow the public's vote in the matter. A few miles up the Mississippi River from St. Louis and with its many hills looking over the large river, Alton had a little of the geographical flavor of San Francisco. The Alton area consisted of several small communities, the largest being Alton itself, "a booming town of three hundred houses . . . fifty stores, four hotels and nine boardinghouses, a bank and two schools."[47] An *Alton Telegraph* editorial reflected pride in the city, saying that the community "presents the most animating appearance. . . . Water Street will present a more imposing and beautiful front than any other of the cities on the western waters. The store houses erected are large, commodious and we might say beautiful. . . . The houses going up in the commercial part of the town are all of the best kind. . . . Between 80 and 100 buildings have been put under contract and commenced this season." It did note "a great want of female society. This is much to be regretted."[48] Lovejoy spoke favorably about the wide streets and good appearance of the community. He noted that "the river here is about one mile wide. A steam ferry boat plies constantly."[49] After a few weeks in Alton, Lovejoy boasted: "The amount of business transacted here is truly astonishing. Seven steam boats were yesterday lying at our landing at one time. . . . We have no means of arriving at the number of inhabitants in Alton, Upper Alton and Middletown, but at a rough estimate, fix at between 2,000 and 4,000."[50]

Some friends had urged Lovejoy to move to Quincy or Jacksonville in Illinois, communities that had stronger antislavery sentiment, but the larger city of Alton appeared to be a better place for a newspaper to succeed financially. Little did he imagine that within a few hours after landing in Alton, he would again be the victim of mob action.

≥ 4

≥ A Press in the River

When Elijah Lovejoy arrived in Alton, he did so with the strong belief that in Illinois there would be more tolerance of antislavery opinions. He had written articles on political questions for the *Alton Telegraph*—not using his name—and there had been little reaction. However, he knew that the majority of people would not share his opinions, for Illinois had been settled from the south to the north, mostly by Southerners. Illinois almost became a slave state, and Alton's location across the river from the slave state of Missouri must have caused him at least a little concern.

Technically, the state into which Lovejoy moved was a free state when it entered the Union in 1818, but in reality, it was only marginally free. When Lovejoy arrived, the official census showed 331 slaves in Illinois; they were slaves who for one reason or another were de facto exempt from the provisions of the Illinois law and state constitution. In addition, there was "practical slavery" of many more in Illinois. These were African Americans who were technically free but who would "voluntarily" lease or rent themselves to someone for a stated period of years. For example, in Gallatin County, "Linda, last out of Missouri Territory," bound herself for ninety-nine years to William Wilson.[1] Linda was approximately nineteen years old when she signed the legal document. Not many of those who signed these documents knew or understood their contents. Such a practice constituted a limited form of slavery.

The will of the first Governor of Illinois, Shadrach Bond, gives some indication of the atmosphere in the "free" state of Illinois: "I give to my loving wife, Achsah Bond, all of my personal property . . . my negro Frank Thomas. . . . I give to my daughter Julia Rachel five hundred dollars and my negro girl Eliza. And to my daughter Achsah Mary five hundred dollars and my negro girl Harriet and to my wife Achsah I give all the rest of my negroes to be disposed of as she thinks best having entire confidence that she will make proper use of it."[2]

As late as sixteen years after Lovejoy's death, 1853, the state of Illinois enacted a law that a free African American entering Illinois could be sold into slavery, a measure sponsored by future Civil War General John A. Logan. In 1862, a referendum passed in Illinois by a margin of 107,650 votes—71 percent to 29 percent—prohibiting any additional African Americans from coming into the state. And in the same year, by a majority of 176,271—86 percent to 14 percent—the people voted to prohibit African Americans from voting or holding office. That year, a free person of African heritage "was arrested for being in the state ten days and intending to remain permanently. He was found guilty and fined. Interested citizens appealed his case to the State Supreme Court, which in 1864 upheld the verdict of the lower court."[3]

Still, Illinois had cities like Quincy and Jacksonville, where strong antislavery sentiment existed. People from these areas gave Lovejoy support, and he hoped for more now that he lived in their state. A few miles from Alton in the small community of Otterville, a free African American named George Washington went to a school established there. He became known in the area as Black George, a respected member of the Otterville community. In Alton itself, or immediately outside the city, at least one free African American family lived. One citizen recalled this period: "I was a boy then and went to day school, boys and girls all together. We had one negro scholar; his name was 'Bill Pitt,' we boys used to use him pretty roughly by one at a time riding on his back at recess, while the other boys whipped up, but like all other negroes at that time he bore it without grumbling."[4]

John Lovejoy, who worked for the *Alton Telegraph*, the new weekly newspaper in the city, felt that his brother's move to bring the *Observer* to Alton would be a good one. Elijah Lovejoy came to the free state of Illinois with hope, a hope that did not last many hours.

The printing press and what other few pieces of printing equipment Lovejoy had salvaged from the wrecking of the plant in St. Louis were shipped on the steamboat *Palmyra* and landed at the wharf in Alton on a Sunday morning in late July 1836. Because he believed it sinful to work on Sunday, Lovejoy had requested that the equipment arrive on another day. Since it came on Sunday, he refused to move it, nor did he want to ask Sunday work of others who would be needed to move it. Instead, he planned to get men to take the heavy equipment to the new *Observer* office early the next morning, but a sad surprise awaited him on Monday morning. During Sunday night's darkness, some men, reportedly from across the river in Missouri, had knocked the press to pieces and thrown it into the river together with his other small pieces of equipment.

News of this destruction spread quickly through Alton, and someone called a meeting of the leading citizens that night. Alton had the reputation of being a law-abiding city, and its citizens expressed outrage at the destruction of Lovejoy's equipment. Those who met that evening spoke of law and order and the need to protect the property of all citizens. The newly elected mayor, John Krum, appeared. The leading businessmen were there, including Winthrop Gilman, a partner of Benjamin Godfrey. Godfrey and Gilman had the largest business in the city, and Godfrey, described by one writer as "a gentleman of large wealth, acquired in fortunate mining investments in some of the Spanish-American colonies,"[5] probably was the wealthiest man in the state. He was a member of the Presbyterian Church. Gilman, a businessman destined to become one of the heroes in the final tragedy, urged that funds be subscribed to get Lovejoy back into the newspaper business, so he might publish a religious newspaper in Alton.

Lovejoy assured them that he was not an Abolitionist, though he did strongly oppose slavery. He told them that he intended primarily to publish a religious newspaper; he felt that he could devote less space to slavery than he did when he lived in St. Louis. "When I was in St. Louis I felt myself called upon to treat at large upon the subject of slavery as I was in a state where the evil existed," he told them. "Now having come to a free state where the evil does not exist, I feel myself less called upon to discuss the subject than when I was in St. Louis." Then he added these significant words: "But, gentlemen, as long as I am an American citizen, and as long as American blood runs in these veins, I shall hold myself at liberty to speak, to write, and to publish whatever I please on any subject."[6]

Lovejoy allowed those at the meeting to get the impression that he would cause no more trouble than any other citizen, that the presence of his *Observer* would not disturb the peace of the city. He had no desire to be a crusader other than in running a religious newspaper that would bring men and women closer to God. What he said impressed them favorably. What remained unsaid was that even in his St. Louis newspaper, slavery had not become the major topic, except in the few months prior to his quick departure. And much as he would deny being an Abolitionist, he would nevertheless be regarded as one because he believed slavery to be wrong and said so. The fine points would not be noticed by people in a frontier society, particularly not by men who might get together over some strong homemade whiskey.

For the moment, however, by the time the meeting finished, Lovejoy had a pledge that he would receive support for his publication. In twelve hours, he had seen his hopes for his newspaper thrown into the river and then revived.

The *Alton Telegraph* characterized the meeting that night as a "respectable assembly." Those at the meeting "came not to express an opinion upon the subject of Abolition, for on that subject there is no difference of opinion amongst us; but they came to give utterance to the abhorrence felt by all for this infamous outrage upon the private property of an individual. He has the right to form his opinions and the right to express them — and the day the right freely to express our own thoughts is taken from us, that day will be the last of our religious and political freedom."[7] The *Telegraph* also agreed to print the *Observer* until a new press arrived.

For his part, John Lovejoy was less optimistic about Alton than his older brother. In fact, he felt "completely disgusted with the West." In a letter home, he added: "You may expect some severe articles one of these days. The people here deserve it, and I think they will get it, for you know that Parish is perfectly able to give them a dose." As to protection for the press coming from Cincinnati, Lovejoy's brother had a glint in his eyes. His plans were simple: "I shall watch it now, and the first person that attempts to come to harm it may expect a small piece of lead to be lodged in him, for it is of no use to trifle with those scoundrels."[8]

In the meantime, in Peoria and in Hennepin in Putnam County, Illinois, Abolitionist leaders had heard about Lovejoy's press being destroyed and urged him to come to their cities. There is no indication Lovejoy ever seriously considered their proposals. Furthermore, back in Alton, no trouble developed. By September of that year, 1836, Lovejoy had the new printing equipment he needed. In his first issue on September 8, he made clear his stand: "The system of Negro slavery is an awful evil and sin." He also clearly stated that under no circumstances would he give up "the rights of conscience, the freedom of opinion, and of the press."

A relatively large newspaper by 1836 frontier standards, the Alton *Observer* focused on religious matters. The first issue's front page had two stories about foreign missions and another urging repentance. Most of the articles about foreign mission work or "The Posture of the Body in Prayer" were not exactly riveting to western citizens, the majority of whom, incidentally, were male; single females did not find the West that attractive.[9]

In his initial Alton edition, Lovejoy published an article displaying the same unfortunate anti-Catholic bias that he had shown earlier in St. Louis: "Charles II [of England] came to an eminently prosperous throne. . . . But Charles was a concealed Roman Catholic. He attempted to introduce his religion—the star of England was instantly darkened."[10] In the first Alton issue on September 8, 1836, Lovejoy also mentioned the "great enlargement of our paper." The editor noted that the paper needed two thousand subscribers to make it a thriving business, and at that time, there were only one thousand. But with almost every issue, he announced a growth in subscriptions.

Occasionally, a story combined religious fervor with other appeal: "A letter from Celeste, the obscene and lascivious danceress . . . states that for the last 90 days, she has received in the cities of New York, Philadelphia, Mobile and New Orleans $26,000. A part of that portion received in New Orleans was earned on evenings of the Sabbath. This is no longer the country of the Pilgrims. Parisian courtesans are paid $26,000 per quarter for the indecent exposure of their persons in public."[11] And in the second Alton issue, he again attacked those who drank alcohol, alienating many more in the hard-drinking city. Almost every edition had at least two temperance articles, with titles like "A Drunkard Saved" and "A Drunkard's Grave." The combination of Catholics and drinkers probably comprised a majority in almost every western community, including Alton. Under the title "The Drunkard's Den," Lovejoy quoted the following opening sentence of a letter from "a correspondent in one of the northern counties of this state": "There is in this village of [taverns] (for there are not less than thirty or forty of these pest houses), a livery stable into which the drunkards retreat when these death-venders wish to get rid of their babbling."[12]

One of the first Alton editions reported that "the mobites" caused the closing of the Negro Sunday school in St. Louis. That edition also stated that the "health of the editor" prevented the newspaper from coming out on time.[13] While Lovejoy's antislavery stand in these early weeks in Alton did not change, it unquestionably was milder than it had been in St. Louis. Lovejoy followed through on his intentions to dwell less on the subject of slavery in the free state of Illinois.

In the meantime, the Lovejoys had moved into a two-story frame home near Second and Cherry Streets in Alton, and they were hoping to lead the normal life of any young married couple with a baby. For several months following the destruction of Lovejoy's press, this appeared possible. Lovejoy continued to be the center of controversy, but to be the center of controversy was better than being the center of mob action. A few weeks after moving to Alton, Lovejoy wrote to his mother: "I can now feel, as I never felt before, the wisdom of Paul's advice not to marry; and yet I would not be without the consolations, which my dear wife and child afford me, for all the world. Still I cannot but feel that it is harder to 'fight valiantly' for the truth, when I risk not only my own comfort, ease, and reputation, and even life, but also that of another beloved one."[14]

Lovejoy's brother John, who now with another brother, Owen, shared Lovejoy's home, continued to be less optimistic than Elijah. Before the new press arrived from Cincinnati, John wrote to his mother: "I do not know as this place is much better [than St. Louis]. The whole country seems to be falling to pieces. But I think there will be a calm after the Presidential election is over." Interestingly, even at this late date in the Lovejoy family thinking, John condemned the Abolitionists. He wrote to his mother: "I am surprised that you should join their standard."[15] Elijah also wrote his mother: "John is well and works steadily in the printing office. He will make a man yet, and one of much usefulness. He is not yet a follower of Jesus, though I will not believe that he will much longer resist the influence of the truth and of God's Spirit." In typical fatherly fashion, Lovejoy described his son: "He is now 13 months old. . . . He is a very healthy, fat large child with blue eyes, rosy cheeks . . . but very intelligent. He does not yet talk, though we are expecting him to commence any day."[16] Discussions of religion continued to dominate almost all correspondence between Elizabeth Lovejoy and her children. John Lovejoy wrote her with a more positive outlook on his religious life than his brother described and added: "You must know . . . that I was guilty of many indiscrete acts in bygone days; but I feel satisfied that I have seen enough of the evil of my ways ever to be guilty of them again."[17]

For some months, Lovejoy's main occupation was getting the *Observer* operating as a successful business, and the evidence suggests that his efforts met with at least modest success. Two months after relocating in Alton, he wrote: "There are four newspapers published weekly [in Alton]—two political, the Spectator and the Telegraph—and two religious, the Observer and the Pioneer. Of these, the Spectator has a circulation of between 200 and 300; the Pioneer about 500; the Telegraph between 700 and 800; and the Observer between 1300 and 1400 copies weekly."[18] Four months later, in March 1837, he could write: "We believe . . . that the Observer is yet destined to survive all its trials. . . . We came into Illinois with less than

1,000 subscribers and we now have more than 1,700."[19] Two months later, he had topped the 2,000 mark.

The newspaper continued to take a somewhat mild tone, even though it stood clearly on the slavery question. For example, the issue of November 3, 1836—a year and four days before Lovejoy's death—appears fairly dull, with perhaps the most exciting item being this notice: "JOB PRINTING—We are prepared to execute this for our friends, in the best style and on the most reasonable terms." But a month later, the lead article dealt with the highly charged slavery question.

An item appeared that soon would result in a more militant stand by the *Observer*. It reported a list of people in the Illinois Synod of the Presbyterian Church who promised support of the newspaper and who pledged themselves for a two-year period to take care of any financial loss Lovejoy might have. Among those who signed the pledge were Dr. Gideon Blackburn, an antislavery leader who would eventually establish Blackburn College in Illinois; Winthrop Gilman, the Alton businessman who had befriended Lovejoy; and Enoch Long, a prominent Alton citizen and businessman, among the few to stand up strongly for Lovejoy during the final days a year later.

No great excitement filled the weeks between this November announcement and New Year's Day. In early December, the *Observer* mentioned Lovejoy as a leader in the Illinois Bible Society, an item anything but controversial. He also taught a Sunday school class regularly. One of his students recalled: "He was my teacher in the Presbyterian Sunday-school, for a time. He was to me like an 'oasis' in the desert of Calvinism, for up to that time, I had heard through Major Hunter, who had been my teacher, a great deal about the 'wrath of God,' but very little about the love of God. Whereas, Mr. Lovejoy, who was of a very loving nature, with fine expression of countenance and a voice as soft and tender as a woman's, talked constantly of the love of God to man."[20]

These first months in Alton—after the first press was thrown into the river—were the only peaceful days Lovejoy would have. Late in January 1837, the Lovejoy tendency to take strong stands showed itself again. He quoted from an antislavery convention held in Ann Arbor, Michigan: "All attempts to justify slavery from the Word of God are gross perversions of its precepts and principle."[21]

Seen by a few, and commented on by many, the militantly antislavery publication the *Emancipator*, in its last edition of 1836, ran a small story favorable to Lovejoy on one of its inside pages, but by March 9, 1837, the journal despised by so many had Lovejoy on its front page. To slavery's supporters, that added dry wood to an already burning flame.

The views Lovejoy expressed more strongly may not seem too exciting or controversial today, but they were in 1836 and 1837, and each strong stand brought death closer. Lovejoy expressed intensely unpopular views, and word by word, he marched toward his death. During the first week of February, he called the idea of sending the slaves back to Africa "utterly inadequate,"[22] a major shift in his position, but he also published letters with differing opinions. Lovejoy editorially opposed a proposal to prohibit distribution of antislavery views, which, it appeared, would pass the Missouri legislature. He called the proposal a threat to a free press. At the same time, he published letters from two Missouri legislators, highly critical of himself. A St. Louis newspaper quoted another Missouri legislator as furious about Lovejoy's antislavery folder, claiming that Lovejoy was encouraging ideas and activities that would end in murder.

At least one of every three issues of the *Observer* had an anti-Catholic article or letter, and sometimes more than one. With inelegant titles like "Popery," Lovejoy fed the prejudices about Roman Catholicism, even as he battled racial prejudices. There is nothing in his writing that shows hostility to Judaism, other than his adherence to a rigid Christianity. And while much of the nation's press editorially denounced Oberlin College in Ohio for their "radical" innovation of accepting both men and women and for teaching them in the same classes, Lovejoy applauded Oberlin for the change. "This has our hearty approval," he wrote. And to salve the religiously offended among his readers, he pointed out: "No one can be admitted to Oberlin who travels on the Sabbath to reach there."[23] Lovejoy did not mention the antislavery leadership that headed Oberlin College, but he probably knew of it.

Barely noticed in the *Observer* was the appointment of the new Illinois attorney general, a man who would play a part in Lovejoy's death. The *Missouri Republican* had more to say about Usher Linder, the new Illinois attorney general, than did the *Observer*. The *Missouri Republican* called him "noisy" and referred indirectly to his heavy drinking, well known in the state capital; the *Republican* simply noted that he was not as "regular in his habits as an Attorney General is expected" to be.[24]

Lovejoy had greater interest in another item in the *Missouri Republican* appearing about this same time. Eleven people on a seventeen-member committee of St. Louis lawyers found Judge Lawless—the man who had encouraged mob action in St. Louis—not suited to serve as a judge. They found him "unfit, by the constitution of his mind, by the intemperance of his feelings, by his impatience in the discharge of official duties."[25] Judge Lawless's actions in the McIntosh murder were at least partially responsible for the action by the St. Louis lawyers. Judge Cranch, in a widely distributed admonition to a grand jury in Washington, D.C., warned of "an increasing contempt of the laws."[26] He specifically cited Judge Lawless's directive to the grand jury in the McIntosh case as an example of justice gone awry, a system of justice that encourages mobs. His eloquent appeal, obviously designed for more than the grand jury he faced, prompted the action by the St. Louis lawyers. Lovejoy undoubtedly found pleasure in seeing his enemy from St. Louis scolded.

Although public hostility to those who opposed slavery mounted in Alton and all over the southern and border states of the nation, it would be wrong to assume that emotional anti-Abolition sentiments were confined to these areas. A mob in Boston almost killed William Lloyd Garrison, the eloquent antislavery leader. The scheduling of three antislavery lectures in Willimantic, Connecticut, caused a riot. Mob action in favor of slavery occurred in states as unlikely as New Hampshire and Maine. Proslavery mobs caused damage in Cincinnati; New York City; Utica, New York; Pontiac, Michigan; Newport, Rhode Island; Ypsilanti, Michigan; and other cities. A popular bowie knife on sale had "Death to Abolition" carved on the blade. In March 1837, in the Illinois House of Representatives, a resolution passed 77–6 supporting slavery in the District of Columbia and criticizing the formation of antislavery societies, youthful Abraham Lincoln being one of the six to vote against the resolution. In Columbia, South Carolina, a large public meeting passed a resolution stating that anyone attacking slavery should be killed. Feelings intensified on both sides everywhere.

Lovejoy sent a copy of the Alton *Observer*, containing a strong antislavery letter from a New York leader, to every member of the Missouri legislature. State Senator R. B. Dawson replied: "I take the liberty to enclosing it back to you. . . . Our branch of the Legislature of Missouri, now in session, have passed a highly penal act for the suppression of the publication, distribution, or promulgation of all such matter; and no doubt exists in my mind, that in due time it will pass the other House, and become a law. . . . You would do well, therefore, to withhold any further publication upon the same subject from the State of Missouri or its citizens." Lovejoy responded editorially: "They might just as well attempt to stop the circulation of the air over their prairies as to prohibit the dissemination of newspapers, whether pro-slavery or anti-slavery, through their mails. People will laugh such a law to scorn. We shall see if the free citizens of Missouri will sanction the principle that their legislature is to decide for them what they shall or what they shall not read."[27]

But as public opposition to Lovejoy grew, so did his courage. In the February 9, 1837, issue of the *Observer*, he took the strongest stand he had taken in Alton. "Two million and a half of our fellow creatures are groaning in bondage, crushed to the earth, deprived of rights which their Maker gave them," he wrote. He ran a story under the title "What is Slavery?" in which he quoted an old slave: "It is to have my back subjected to the cowhide or the cart-whip, at the will or caprice of my master or any of his family. Every child has a right to curse or kick or cuff the old man. . . . Not one cent of what I earn is or can be my own. It is to depart my hut every morning, with the sickening fear that before I return at night, it will be visited by the slave-driving fiend. It is to return at night and find my worst fears realized—my first-born son, denied even the poor privilege of bidding his father farewell, is on his way, a chained and manacled victim . . . to a distant market, where human flesh is bought and sold. It is to enter my cabin,· and see my wife or daughter struggling in the lustful embraces of my master, or some of his white friends, without daring to attempt their rescue. . . . Should I open my lips to protest, a hundred lashes would be the consequence; and should I raise my hand to hit the brutal wretch, death would be the price."

In earlier issues, Lovejoy had said that slavery was a sin. Now he went one step further and said that those who do not fight slavery—the large majority of citizens—"are fighting against God." Without identifying it, Lovejoy cited one city where "there are no female slaves over the age of twenty who have not been sexually violated." His fellow ministers were a special target. He condemned those who "preach against intemperance and Sabbath breaking, against covetousness and murder, and yet pass over slavery in silence." As a minister, Lovejoy said that he had the obligation to preach against slavery at "whatever risk" and that a minister has the duty to speak "in behalf of more than two million of my fellow beings who are not permitted to open their mouths to plead their own cause." He added: "I have lived about eight years in a slave state and except in one or two instances, I do not recall ever having heard slaveholders, whether in or out of church, criticized for neglecting or abusing their slaves. At the same time I have seen the slaves sitting out on the carriage box, through all the service, while their masters and mistresses, whom they drove to church, were worshipping with great devoutness within."[28]

When a reader in Missouri complained about too much antislavery material in the *Observer*, Lovejoy wrote to him: "If I could hold my peace on this subject with a clear conscience, I would most assuredly do it. My course has cost me many a valued friend. But I cannot, and I am sure you do not ask or wish a Christian to connive at what he believes to be sin, for the sake of popularity."[29] This reader, Major G. C. Sibley of Linden Wood, Missouri, who had befriended Lovejoy in earlier Missouri difficulties, replied by canceling his subscription and complaining about the terrible insults to "the many thousands of Christians who like myself entertain opinions on several subjects different from yours."[30]

In most respects, however, Lovejoy's life during these months was a normal one. He became the first minister of a new Presbyterian church that started in Upper Alton, and he had time occasionally to teach a Sunday school class at the larger Alton church, the First Presbyterian. The members of the church he served as a minister were mostly farmers. Lovejoy, who had known farm life from childhood on, could speak the language they understood.

Some of the money that had been pledged by Alton citizens for the *Observer* was not coming in, however, and Lovejoy had no choice but to take out a loan for four hundred dollars, a sizable sum in 1837. To help with the money problems, Celia Ann had a few boarders who received their meals somewhat regularly at their home. A Lutheran minister stayed with them during the winter. Their financial situation became so bad that for a short period Lovejoy had to sell clothing and hardware items door to door. And increasingly, he found that the people who helped him were the Abolitionists.

As he leaned more on the Abolitionists for financial help for his newspaper, he became more outspoken in his stand against slavery. Most of the new subscribers were Abolitionists. Lovejoy knew through his experience with the *St. Louis Times*, the first newspaper he edited in St. Louis, that if he ran a noncontroversial publication with no mention of slavery, he could do well financially. Nevertheless, he chose to follow his convictions even though it meant losing money. The fact that antislavery people were coming more and more to his aid encouraged him and gave him time to devote to the editorial side of the newspaper instead of the business end.

When he consulted with those who had financed the *Observer*'s rebirth in Alton regarding his strong antislavery stand, they gave him their full approval. As one of his friends noted: "He was advised by Mr. Gilman to follow the dictates of his own judgment, which he accordingly did."[31] This support came despite the fact that so many in Alton viewed Lovejoy as a New Englander with strange ways and views and a strange accent in a population mostly southern in background.

In 1837, the nation's economy dipped dramatically. People were out of work. Businesses closed. The public in Alton was not as aware of the national trends as people would be in a later day. They did know that business in Alton was getting worse and that more Alton citizens faced unemployment. Lovejoy said God caused the recession as a punishment for sin, but the people in Alton saw it in a different light. Rumors spread that this strange New Englander, Elijah Lovejoy, bore part of the blame, and people began wondering what could be done to stop him. Alton soon would be as dangerous for Lovejoy as St. Louis.

Monument at the site of the birthplace of
Elijah Lovejoy in Albion, Maine, photograph by
Phillip G. Dow, Sr.

Elijah Lovejoy, silhouette.
(Reprinted by permission, Missouri
Historical Society.)

Lovejoy's house in Alton, wood engraving by Louis Hofman. (Reprinted by permission, Missouri Historical Society.)

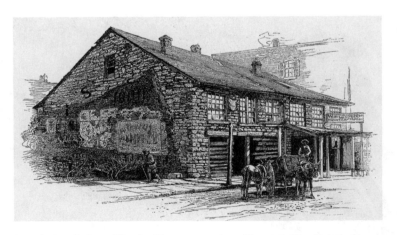

Lovejoy's printing office in Alton, engraving. (Reprinted by permission, Missouri Historical Society.)

Alton, Illinois, watercolor by Henry Lewis, 1848. (Reprinted by permission, Missouri Historical Society.)

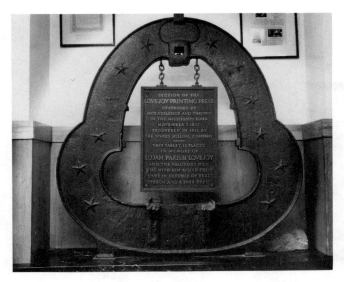

Section of Lovejoy's printing press, photograph by Jill Sherman. (Reprinted by permission, Missouri Historical Society.)

Proslavery riot of November 7, 1837, wood engraving, 1837. (Reprinted by permission, Missouri Historical Society.)

Lovejoy memorial plate. (Reprinted by permission, Lovejoy Library, Southern Illinois University at Edwardsville.)

Lovejoy monument in Alton, photograph by Robert Graul. (Courtesy Alton
Museum of History and Art.)

❧ 5

❧ Danger and Violence

The fourth of July in 1837, the sixty-first anniversary of the signing of the Declaration of Independence, was a day of big celebration in Alton and in the rest of the United States. People joined in a combination of speeches, flag waving, shouting, and drinking. Everyone appeared to be having a great time — with one exception. In his office, Lovejoy wrote an editorial: "What bitter mockery is this. We assemble to thank God for our own freedom, and to eat and drink with joy and gladness of heart, while our feet are on the necks of nearly three millions of our fellow men. Not all our shouts of self-congratulation can drown their groans. Even that very flag of freedom that waves over their heads is formed from materials cultivated by slaves, on a soil moistened with their blood."[1]

That, many felt, went too far! The *Observer* came out on Saturday, and on Tuesday night, someone called a meeting of citizens. A few at the meeting had been drinking heavily before it started. The combination of aroused anger and heavy drinking sometimes can strike terror in a community, but in this instance, the mixture resulted only in confusion. Nothing came of the gathering except the agreement to hold another meeting the following week.

One editorial had not prompted the meeting. Month by month and issue by issue, Lovejoy had become more vehement in his antislavery statements. Some of the encouragement to Lovejoy came from his family. His mother wrote: "God had a great work for you to do and he seems to have called you into the field of action."[2] Lovejoy's brother Joseph sent a fifty-dollar contribution. Two other brothers, Owen and John, lived with him and did nothing to slow Lovejoy. As early as April, Lovejoy wrote to his brother Joseph that the *Observer* "is prospering, gaining favor with man, and I hope with God." He added: "I know not what may be before me."[3]

Moreover, for several months, Lovejoy had been hinting at the need for an Illinois Antislavery Society. In March, he noted that one had been formed in Pennsylvania, with "the most respectable citizens of the state" participating.[4] He wrote that an "antislavery society had been formed, on an average, every day for the last two years in the United States."[5] Soon he reported on a meeting of the Adams County Antislavery Society in Quincy, Illinois, at the Congregational church there, in which they adopted a resolution to "rely mainly on prayer . . . for the removal of slavery" and added as part of the resolution: "We earnestly invite every female in our land who sincerely desires to sustain God's holy law, the honor of her sex, and the happiness of the human family, to unite their prayers and efforts for the emancipation of our brethren and sisters from bondage."[6] Women, whose rights were extremely limited, sometimes had greater insight than men into the injustice of slavery.

In the same issue that carried the plainspoken Fourth of July message, Lovejoy ran an editorial entitled "Illinois Antislavery Society." He stated: "Is it not time that such a society be formed? We would do nothing rashly, but it does seem to us that the time to form such a society has fully come. We shall hope to have a response from the friends of the slave without delay." Then he added that he already was regarded as a "fanatic" by many and that he felt he "must become more and more vile in their eyes." He also said he had "never felt enough, nor prayed enough, nor done enough in behalf of the perishing slave."[7] This served notice to a population already aroused that he would provide leadership in forming an Antislavery Society and that his stand on slavery would become stronger in the future, not weaker. He also wrote to the man he once despised, William Lloyd Garrison, asking for help.

Lovejoy reached the conclusion that "the work of abolishing slavery has to be done, chiefly, in the free states. In the slave state the church has as a body gone heartily into the business of buying and selling their fellow men, and their ministers generally have gone with them."[8] He made his appeals primarily to the religious community: "Why are the ears of so many good brethren so sensitive to the cry which comes to them from the perishing heathen on the other side of the world, while yet they remain insensible to the dying groans of heathen in our midst? There is a strange inconsistency in this."

However, the majority of items in Lovejoy's newspaper still were not about slavery. He took time to note with displeasure that a theater was being built in Chicago: "It will be a long time, we are apt to think, before such an establishment will get a foothold in Alton. We build churches instead of theaters." He continued to attack the drinking of liquor. In that cause, he received support from A. W. Corey, editor of the *Temperance Herald*, nationally circulated but printed in Alton. Lovejoy occasionally attended temperance meetings.

Changing conditions in cotton production and marketing made slaves more and more valuable. As the price of a slave went up, so did the slaveholder's desire to retain the system. Opponents of slavery like Lovejoy were perceived as trying to take away "property" growing in value, and this perception intensified the animosity between proslavery and antislavery people. At the border of a slave state and a free state, Alton found itself caught in the middle of this chasm in people's feelings.

On July 11, 1837, some people held a second public meeting,

in a place called the Market House, to determine what to do about Lovejoy, a meeting that the *Alton Telegraph* reported as being made up of "a large and respectable concourse of the citizens."[9] Those at the meeting said they were friends of the *Observer* who wanted to stop antislavery talk in the newspaper. At this meeting, several complained that Lovejoy had violated his pledge. When he came to Alton, they asserted, he said he would not make the *Observer* an Abolitionist newspaper. Now he openly and aggressively pushed the antislavery cause. The charge had enough truth to convince the proslavery people and perhaps some who had no strong feelings. Although when he had first come to Alton, Lovejoy had believed he could follow a moderate course, he also made clear at the time that he reserved his freedom to say what he wanted on any subject, this being his right as an American citizen. As he studied the matter and as slavery became an increasing national concern, Lovejoy devoted more and more space to the issue in easy-to-understand words, but to the proslavery crowd, he was a "nigger-loving preacher who broke his word."

Those at the July 11 meeting made clear that they were not trying to make a slave state out of the free state of Illinois, but neither were they going to tolerate antislavery talk from a man who had "broken his word." To let Lovejoy continue to publish would be "cowardly," said Dr. J. A. Halderman, the chairman of the meeting and a respected physician.[10] His words brought cheers. A resolution carefully drafted prior to the meeting passed. It said that those at the meeting opposed "all violence and mobs"; however, they requested of Lovejoy "a discontinuance of the publication of his incendiary doctrines which alone have a tendency to disturb the quiet of our citizens and neighbors."[11] They appointed a committee of five, plus the chair, to see Lovejoy about the resolutions they had passed. The committee decided that instead of seeing him personally, they would send him a copy of the minutes of the meeting, together with a letter, asking him to reply.

If they had hoped for meek agreement on Lovejoy's part, they were in for a disappointment. Lovejoy told them that he could not bow to their wishes without admitting the death of liberty of the press and freedom of speech. Some Lovejoy supporters believed he erred in not rebutting a charge that he had made "a solemn pledge of silence" when he came to Alton. Their statement referred to that, and Lovejoy, by not addressing it, may have lent believability to the charge that he had violated a pledge. After going into the free speech issue in some detail in his response, he said: "Gentlemen, I have confidence you will, upon reflection, agree with me."[12] Of course, they did not. Lovejoy did say he would be glad to print letters to the editor opposing his views. It became clear that something stronger than a resolution of citizens at a public meeting would be needed to stop him.

Lovejoy took the mounting tension in stride, but his wife could not. A sensitive person by nature, the emotional storms that surrounded her husband frightened Celia Ann Lovejoy. These worked on her nervous system so that she became seriously ill. When word of this spread around Alton, it was soon topped with an exciting rumor. Lovejoy, the rumor ran, had announced in the new Presbyterian Church in Upper Alton that if his wife died, he would marry an African American. This false story quickly passed throughout the area.

Late in July 1837, Lovejoy finally identified himself completely with the Abolitionists. He had slowly been moving in that direction. First he saw no great evil in slavery; then he favored returning some blacks to Africa and freeing others gradually; now he believed in immediate freedom for all slaves. Thirteen months earlier, he had taken a turn toward Abolitionism. An officer of the National Antislavery Society wrote to him, asking the newspaper to provide names of people willing to join in an effort to get Congress to abolish slavery in the District of Columbia. Lovejoy published the letter and commented: "The United States Government has no right to interfere with slavery in the States, but it can and ought to forbid it in the District of Columbia."[13] At that point, he was not yet an Abolitionist, but he accepted the idea for the District of Columbia.

His July 1837 editorial shifted all the way. He wrote: "In respect to the subject now to be discussed, the writer confesses no one of his readers can possibly be more prejudiced, or more hostile to antislavery measures or men, than he once was." The editorial identified Lovejoy with the Abolitionists and defended them. He called slavery a SIN in capital letters. He said profiting from the work that a slave had done was robbery. Then in his editorial enthusiasm, he said that "more than half" of those who attack Abolitionists as "amalgamationists" (those advocating interracial marriage) "actually practice amalgamation themselves," that is, that the majority of the male critics of Abolitionism have at one time or another violated African American women. His editorial also noted a sensitive fact: "Thousands hold as slaves their own sons and daughters, and brothers and sisters."[14]

Lovejoy responded on that most sensitive of issues as part of an answer to religious periodicals around the nation. He had emerged as a second-tier spokesperson for the antislavery cause, not as prominent as some, but increasingly listened to. The *Baptist Banner* of Louisville wrote: "The Abolitionists are beginning everywhere to throw off the mask, and boldly to advocate . . . the intermarriage of whites and blacks! . . . the union of persons that God . . . has put asunder, as much as he had separated midnight from noonday."[15] Lovejoy replied: "We read most of the Abolition publications in the land, and we have never seen any such position taken by any one of them. . . . But if God has put the black and white so far asunder, how happens it that they come together so readily in the state where you live? . . . Go into the streets of Louisville, where there are no Abolitionists, and tell me how many individuals among all the coloured population that throng your streets you can find whose faces shine with the pure gloss of an African complexion. Such persons are about as scarce in St. Louis as black swans are on the Mississippi, and we suspect the case is pretty similar in Louisville."[16] And to publications that were silent or worse, like the *Christian Mirror*, he wrote bluntly: "You seem to me to not at all . . . understand your responsibilities in relation to the subject of Slavery."[17]

On another occasion, he wrote: "We are glad to see slaveholders treating their slaves with kindness, teaching them to read the Bible (which however, they hardly ever do), sending them to the Sabbath school and the church. But what we are protesting against is the idea that the gospel is satisfied and its precepts fulfilled when these things . . . are done. If you rob a man of ten dollars, it is better that you should spend the money in disseminating copies of the Bible, than of Tom Paine's Age of Reason; but doing the former will not more justify the original theft than the latter."[18]

Early in August, shortly before the next violent incident, the Madison County Antislavery Society organized in Alton. Everyone knew that Lovejoy, who served as organization chairman, bore the responsibility for getting it started. Antislavery societies were not exactly sweeping the state, even in the regions more remote from the slave state of Missouri. The August 17, 1837, issue of the *Emancipator* reported a grand total of three societies in the entire state of Illinois, the largest with forty-two members. Lovejoy knew that he would not receive a warm welcome in Alton for this leadership.

Public opinion escalated—and not just among the less educated element. Lovejoy's rising national role annoyed the citizens of Alton, and two candidates for mayor of Alton said they did not believe Lovejoy had a right to publish his newspaper. At one point, a group of twelve citizens, including four physicians, schemed to tar and feather Lovejoy and carry him through town. The idea was to make him appear so ridiculous that he would voluntarily leave the city. After carrying him through town, they would have a canoe ready at the edge of the Mississippi where they would put him adrift. By the time he got back, the paper would be late, and the whole town would be laughing at him. They planned to catch Lovejoy at night, when he walked home. The original group of twelve soon swelled to a larger gathering. Lovejoy related what happened next:

> About 9 o'clock I was returning from a friend's where I had been to marry a couple. I stepped into the apothecary's as I came through town and got some medicine to bring home to my wife, she being very sick. . . .
>
> We reside more than half a mile from town. And just as I was leaving the principal street I met the mob. They did not at first recognize me, and I parted their columns for some distance, and had just reached the rear, when some of them began to suspect who I was. They immediately came after me. I did not hurry at all, believing a man in my position should not flee.
>
> They seemed a little reluctant to come up to me, and I could hear their leaders swearing at them, and telling them to push on. By this time they began to throw clods of dirt at me and several hit, without hurting me. And now a fellow pushed up to my side armed with a club, to see for sure who it was. He then yelled out: "It's the damned Abolitionist; give him hell." Then there was another rush at me. But when they got close, they seemed to fall back again.
>
> Finally a number of them linked themselves together arm in arm, pushed by me and wheeled in the road before me, stopping me completely. I asked why they stopped me. By this time the cry was all around me, "Damn him!" "Rail him!" "Tar and feather him!"
>
> I had no doubt that such was to be my fate. I then said to them, "I have one request to make of you, and then you may do with me what

you please." I then asked them to send one of their group to take the medicine to my wife, which I begged them to do without alarming her. This they promised to do, and sent one man to do it, who did it like they promised.

I then said to them, "You had better let me go home. You have no right to detain me. I have never injured you."

They began to curse and swear, when I added, "I am in your hands, and you must do with me whatever God permits you to do."

They consulted with each other for a few moments and then told me I could go home.[19]

During their brief discussion, one of the members of the group, a Southerner, said, "Boys, I can't lay my hand upon as brave a man as this."

Later that same evening, two of the physicians who were part of the gathering awakened one of the local attorneys, George Davis, and asked him to represent them in case Lovejoy should sue. Lovejoy had recognized both of them, and they were temporarily frightened by the possibility of legal action. Lovejoy did nothing against them, however. They soon recovered from their fright and were among the leaders of the mob that killed Lovejoy less than three months after this early night encounter.

Lovejoy made it home safely, but not all was quiet in Alton that night. Earlier in August, rumors spread that a mob would invade the *Observer* office. The printers had heard the rumor and brought guns to the office. On one night, the guns frightened away a few men who appeared determined to do damage. A second time, heavy rains dampened the attempt at mob violence. By this time, Benjamin Godfrey, the leading businessman in Alton who had helped bring Lovejoy to Alton, regretted he became involved in the whole affair. When he heard about the printers bringing guns to defend the equipment, he feared for the merchandise he had in the same building. He asked them to take the guns home. This they did.

On the same night of August 21 when the small group of men stopped Lovejoy, people broke into the *Observer* office. The intruders probably were the same men who had planned to tar and feather Lovejoy. Apparently during the few minutes of consultation with one another after the encounter with Lovejoy, they decided that instead of hurting Lovejoy, with an ill wife, they would damage the printing office. What time of night they entered the printing plant is not known, but they broke the large printing press into pieces and tossed it into the river. It was the second time that this had happened in Alton.

At least part of the blame for this second destruction of the press in Alton can be placed on the *Missouri Republican* of St. Louis, which had many readers in Alton. One editorial stated: "The editor of the *Observer* has merited the full measure of the community's indignation; and if he will not learn from experience, they are very likely to teach him by practice, something of the light in which the honorable and respectable portion of the community view his conduct. He has forfeited all claims to the protection of that or any other community by his continued efforts to promote antislavery doctrines."[20] Four days before people destroyed the second press, the *Missouri Republican* came out with another editorial that all but called for illegal action: "We had hoped that our neighbors would have ejected from amongst them that minister of mischief, the *Observer. . . .* Something must be done in this matter, and that speedily! The good people of Illinois must either put a stop to the efforts of those fanatics, or expel them from their community."[21]

After the anti-Lovejoy zealots destroyed Lovejoy's second press, the *Missouri Republican* confidently predicted that the *Observer* would no longer appear in Alton, and it did not condemn the illegal action: "We learn from Alton that the materials of the Observer office . . . were completely destroyed. . . . He [Lovejoy] would not, it seems, stop or change

his course, and he . . . has been made to pay for his obstinacy."
It said the community actions "were made necessary by his
indiscreet course."[22] The next day a news report from Alton in the
Missouri Republican described those who destroyed Lovejoy's
equipment as "orderly" and editorialized that the mob action
"will be used for the purpose of injuring the reputation of our
neighboring town. This would be unjust in the extreme." In
response to the *Missouri Republican*, the *Peoria Register* said:
"It strikes us as exceedingly impolitic in the public press to speak
of outrages of this kind with anything like favor. Do not those
who countenance and cheer them on see that they may themselves one day incur the resentment of the mob?"[23] The next
issue of the Peoria newspaper on September 9 observed: "If the
sympathy felt for Mr. Lovejoy elsewhere equals that expressed
for him by his friends here, he will soon have another press at his
command, with double his late list of subscribers. We grant that
mobs may put down the objects of their dislike in the slave states,
but they only elevate them higher in the free ones."

Four days after the press had been destroyed, the *Missouri
Republican* continued to comment favorably on the illegal action, its Alton correspondent noting that "a large concourse
witnessed the proceedings" and concluding: "You may confidently assure our friends and the public that abolitionism is now
at an end in Alton. For many weeks past, the public have been in a
state of feverish excitement in consequence of Mr. Lovejoy's
continued publication of these doctrines, regardless of the per-
suasions of our citizens. All now is quiet and [in] good order."[24]

Also in St. Louis, the *Missouri Argus* suggested that Lovejoy
"deserved" what happened and noted: "This terminates the
existence of a print which has for a long time been disseminating
doctrines peculiarly hurtful to the domestic institutions of this
State—a State in which the Observer has a wide circulation,
notwithstanding its bad tendency. . . . The people of Alton are

opposed to a disturbance of the domestic relations of States when the sanctity of those relations is guaranteed by the Constitution of the United States." That unusual editorial twist—using the Constitution to uphold suppression of free speech—concluded by noting that "working people of all the free States will stand by the Constitution of their country and sustain the institutions [i.e., slavery] solemnly guaranteed by that sacred instrument."[25]

The *Alton Telegraph* called the destruction of printing supplies and equipment an "OUTRAGE" in capital letters,[26] but this resulted in an anonymous threat to destroy the press and printing equipment of the *Telegraph*.[27]

Three days after the destruction of the second press in Alton, John Lovejoy wrote to the owners of the *Quincy Argus*, asking if it would be for sale. Whether John wrote on his own behalf or for his brother is uncertain.

As it became clearer and clearer that public opinion in Alton opposed Lovejoy, the well intentioned but weak started to desert him. Ministers who quietly had been standing up for Lovejoy now tended openly to take the solid, middle-of-the-road approach and "wash their hands" of the whole affair. "Both sides are wrong," they said. Businessmen who had thought the new publication would be one more solid business for the city were now either hostile or frightened into silence. The *Alton Spectator* openly sided with those who called for action. The *Alton Telegraph* said it would not "interfere or meddle in any way."[28]

By this time, the *Observer* had become more popular around the nation, and Lovejoy had gone far past the two thousand subscribers he said he needed to make the business a success. He still had financial difficulties, however, caused in particular by people who owed him money. He finally started publishing items like the following: "Mr. Rhodolphus Lamb of Delhi, Green[e] County, has left the place owing us $150 and gone we know not where." At the end of a list of such items, he added: "This list will be continued if need be. We have suffered in silence long enough."[29] Despite these financial difficulties, the *Observer* increased in national stature and popularity. Contributions and subscriptions grew, as did people who encouraged the battling editor. Isaac Gallard of Commerce, Illinois, wrote a typical letter: "It is truly mortifying to the feelings of every honorable minded American citizen to learn that any portion of this community are so lost to every sense of propriety and self-respect, as to disgrace themselves by such acts [of harassment against Lovejoy]."[30] He said he would send fifty dollars within sixty days. Lovejoy received over fifty letters supporting him after his foes destroyed his second press. But from Petersburg, Illinois, Spencer Merrill wrote: "One number of your paper has come to hand. . . . I was induced to subscribe for it. Since I have seen one number, I am fully determined never to take another out of the office. . . . You may discontinue it—I never will pay for it, and the only wish I have upon the subject is that you, your press and agent were all in hell."[31] Lovejoy printed the letter.

When his opponents destroyed the second press, Lovejoy issued an appeal to his subscribers, printed by the *Alton Telegraph*, asking for fifteen hundred dollars to replace the second press that had been thrown in the river. Lovejoy wrote: "If you will sustain me, by the help of God, the press shall be again established at this place, and shall be sustained, come what will. Let the experiment be fairly tried, whether the liberty of speech and of the press is to be enjoyed in Illinois or not."[32] In a short time, the money came in, and Lovejoy ordered a new press.

After the destruction of the second press, Lovejoy began to have serious doubts about what he should do. The Alton business leaders who had financed his newspaper were his special concern because he knew that many of them were unhappy with the position in which Lovejoy had placed them. A tract widely distributed in Alton, written by a Rev. James Smiley of Mississippi, also influenced some of his supporters, dampening their ardor. Written in response to an antislavery statement issued by the presbytery of Chillicothe, Missouri, the tract made the case for biblical support of the American system of slavery, and it was written well enough to have an impact on a deeply divided city. Lovejoy also had friends who, though as stoutly opposed to slavery as he, felt that he had done all the good he could in Alton and that it might be wise to move on and let someone with fewer enemies continue the battle.

Lovejoy wrote to his friends and to the owners of the newspaper: "Having learned that there is a division among you, as to the propriety of my continuing to fill the office of the editor of the Alton *Observer*, I do not hesitate a moment to submit the question to your decision. Most cheerfully will I resign my post, if in your collective wisdom, you think the cause we all profess to love will thereby be promoted."[33] He asked as the condition for his leaving that the debts he had accumulated be paid. These supporters had a divided opinion. He asked for a unanimous vote as to what his course should be; when no unanimous vote occurred—and he probably knew it would not—he did what he felt duty compelled him to do: stay on as editor.

Lovejoy knew the intensity of the hatred toward him. When he made his decision to stay, the third press was on its way. It arrived from Cincinnati on September 21, 1837, exactly one month after the second press had been destroyed. Lovejoy did not happen to be in Alton at the time. Several of his friends gathered at the river's edge to see that the press arrived safely at the Gerry and Weller warehouse. Alton's new and youthful mayor, John M. Krum, put in an appearance. He saw the citizens protecting the press and heard a few cries of "There goes the Abolitionist press; stop it!," but no violence occurred. Throughout the incidents that happened during these months, twenty-seven-year-old Mayor Krum stood on the side of the law, though never strongly enough to be fully effective. The mayor told Lovejoy's friends that he would see that the city protected the press.

Lovejoy's supporters took the mayor at his word and left the scene. Mayor Krum assigned a constable to watch at the door of the warehouse. The constable's orders were to watch the warehouse until near midnight. As soon as the constable left, ten or twelve men with handkerchiefs over their faces broke into the warehouse, rolled the press (still in its crate) to the river bank, broke it into pieces, and threw it into the Mississippi. The mayor arrived at the scene before all the damage had been done and ordered them to disperse. They told Mayor Krum that they were busy and that if he wanted to avoid personal harm, he had better go home. This he did.

The *Alton Telegraph* reported: "The store-house of Messrs. Gerry and Weller, on Second Street, was forcibly entered by twenty or thirty persons, who proceeded . . . to carry off a box containing a press . . . and after totally destroying it, threw the fragments into the river."[34] At the Illinois state capital, the *Peoria Register* commented: "As unpardonable as is the conduct of the abolitionist Lovejoy . . . the remedy sought against him and his press is less pardonable. . . . Apart from its illegality, we doubt even the policy of putting down this abolition press by violence." And then the newspaper added inaccurately: "Look at the late letter of Mr. Lovejoy. The putting down his press was made by him the pretext for demanding more money from his friends. . . . His letter shows also it comes from a man governed less by principle than avarice."[35] The Galena *Gazette and Advertiser* observed: "The premeditated destruction of Mr. Lovejoy's office will make more abolitionists in one month than it could have done in two years [of publishing]."[36]

The *Western Adventurer* of Iowa asked: "Can the citizens of Alton allow this act of lawless desperation to go unpunished? If so—then none of her citizens are safe."[37] Even the *Missouri Republican* tempered its enthusiasm for lawlessness slightly, observing: "It is now generally believed that Mr. Lovejoy will not in [the] future persist in the reestablishment of an abolition press in Alton. . . . We regret, exceedingly, these violations of the law and if Mr. Lovejoy has any regard for himself, he will not continue the unequal contest. If he continues to provoke these attacks, they may terminate more disastrously than the mere destruction of property."[38]

Mayor Krum offered a one-hundred-dollar award "for the apprehension and conviction" of the offenders—not for information leading to their arrest and conviction.[39] It was a safe offer. For the average citizen to apprehend and get a conviction was extremely unlikely, as the mayor knew.

Celia Ann Lovejoy understandably became almost hysterical in the midst of all this. Their little boy had become sick, and now Celia Ann was in the third month of her second pregnancy and uncomfortably ill, though not in a serious condition. The first pregnancy had been difficult for her, and the second followed the same pattern.

Lovejoy himself did not feel well and decided to take his family to Celia Ann's home in St. Charles, where he had an invitation from Rev. William Campbell to preach at the large Presbyterian church. Perhaps a few days of rest at St. Charles would be helpful, he thought. Lovejoy related what happened on Sunday:

> I preached in the morning and at night. After the audience was dismissed at night, a young man came in, and passing by me, slipped the following note into my hand: "Mr. Lovejoy, be watchful as you come from the church tonight. A Friend."
>
> We received no molestation on our way, and the whole matter passed from my mind. Brother Campbell and I sat conversing for nearly an hour; Mrs. Lovejoy had gone to another room and lain

down; her mother was with her, having our sick child, while an unmarried sister of Mrs. Lovejoy was in the room with Mr. Campbell and myself. The access to the rooms is by a flight of stairs. About 10 o'clock I heard a knocking at the foot of the stairs. The knocking woke up Mrs. Lovejoy and her mother, who inquired what was wanted. The answer was, "We want to see Mr. Lovejoy; is he in?" To this I answered myself, "Yes, I am here."

Two of them came into the room and grabbed me. I asked what they wanted. "We want you downstairs, damn you," was the reply. They commenced to pull me out of the house.

Not succeeding immediately, one of them began to beat me with his fists.

By this time Mrs. Lovejoy had come into the room. In doing so she had to make her way through the mob on the portico, who attempted to hinder her from coming by rudely pushing her back, and one "chivalrous" southerner actually drew his dagger on her. Her only reply was to strike him in the face with her hand, and then rushing past him, she flew to where I was, and throwing her arms around me, she boldly faced the mobites, with a fortitude and self-devotion which none but a woman and a wife ever displayed. While they were attempting with oaths and curses to drag me from the room, she was hitting them in the face with her hands, or clinging to me to aid in resisting their efforts, and telling them they must first take her before they should have her husband. Her energetic measures, seconded by those of her mother and sister, induced the assailants to let me go and leave the room.

As soon as they were gone, Mrs. Lovejoy's powers of endurance failed her and she fainted. So soon as she had recovered from her fainting she relapsed into hysterical fits, moaning and shrieking and calling upon my name alternately.

Mrs. Lovejoy's health is at all times extremely delicate, and at present peculiarly so, she being some months advanced in pregnancy. Her situation at this time was truly alarming and distressing. To add to the perplexities of the moment, I had our sick child in my arms, taken up from the floor where he had been left by his grandmother, in the hurry and alarm of the first onset of the mob.

While I was endeavoring to calm Mrs. Lovejoy's dreadfully excited mind, the mob returned, breaking into the room and rushing to the bedside, again attempting to force me from the house. The brutal wretches were totally indifferent to her heart-rending cries and shrieks — she was far too exhausted to move; and I suppose they would have succeeded in forcing me out had not my friend William M. Campbell (the Presbyterian minister) at this juncture come in and with undaunted boldness assisted me.

Others aided forcing the mob from the room, so that the house was now clear a second time. The mob did not, however, leave the yard of the house, which was full of drunken wretches uttering the most awful and soul-chilling oaths and imprecations, and swearing they would have me at all hazards.

One fellow seemed the most bent on my destruction. He did not appear to be drunk, but both in words and actions appeared almost fiendish. He was telling a story to the mobites which was just calculated to madden them. His story was that his wife had recently been violated by a Negro. This he said was all my fault, that I had instigated the Negro to do the deed. He was a ruined man, he said, and would just as soon die, but before he died he "would have my blood."

The mob now rushed up the stairs a third time, and one of them, a David Knott of St. Charles, came in with a note which required me to send them a written answer. This I at first declined, but yielding to their urgent advice, I took my pencil and wrote: "I have already taken my passage in the state to leave tomorrow morning at least by 9 o'clock." This at first seemed to pacify them. They went away, as I supposed, finally. But after having visited the taverns they returned with increased fury and violence. My friends now became thoroughly alarmed. They joined in advising me to escape should an opportunity occur.

I was at length compelled by the united entreaties of them all, especially of my wife, to consent to do so. Accordingly, when the efforts of those below had diverted the attention of the mob for a few minutes, I left the house and went away unnoticed.

It was now about midnight. I walked about a mile to a friend's residence. He kindly furnished me with a horse; and having rested myself on the sofa an hour or two, for I was exhausted, I rode to Mr. Watson's, another friend, where I arrived about daybreak, four miles from town. Here Mrs. Lovejoy, though exhausted and utterly unfit to leave her bed, joined me in the morning, and we came home, reaching Alton about noon. We met no hindrance, though Mrs. Lovejoy was constantly alarmed with fears of pursuit from St. Charles.

On our arrival in Alton, as we were going to our house, almost the first person we met in the street was one of the very men who had first broken into our house at St. Charles. Mrs. Lovejoy instantly recognized him and at once became greatly alarmed.

There was reason for fear, since the mob in St. Charles had repeatedly declared their determination to pursue me and to take my life. One of them, the man who told the story, boasted that he was chasing me and that he had assisted in destroying my press in Alton.

When these facts were known to my friends, they thought it advisable that our house should be guarded on Monday night. Indeed this was necessary to quiet Mrs. Lovejoy's fears. Though completely exhausted from the scenes of the night before, she could not rest. Her moments of fitful slumber were continually interrupted with cries of alarm. This continued all the afternoon and evening of Monday, and I began to entertain serious fears of the consequences. As soon, however, as our friends—ten of them— arrived with arms, her fears subsided, and she sank into a comparatively silent sleep which continued through most of the night.

We have no one with us tonight, except the members of our own family. A loaded musket is standing at my bedside while my two brothers in an adjoining room have three others together with pistols, cartridges, etc. And this is the way we live in Alton.[40]

Even the *Missouri Republican*, after reporting the St. Charles incident, observed about Lovejoy: "Unless caught in some . . . act of offence to our laws, his person should be protected."[41]

6

Prelude to Death

Lovejoy traveled to Jacksonville, about seventy miles north of Alton, for a visit with his friend, Rev. Edward Beecher, president of Illinois College. Beecher and two others had been tried for heresy in the local presbytery in 1833 for "their liberal theology." Central to the charge was their antislavery stand. The presbytery acquitted them.[1] One of the most prominent men in the state to openly take an antislavery stand, Beecher encouraged Lovejoy in the newspaper's forthright position.

The two discussed the calling of a state antislavery convention in Alton. In 1833, a National Antislavery Convention had been held in Philadelphia. Its platform read: "We shall organize antislavery societies if possible in every city, town, and village in the land. We shall send forth agents to lift up the voice of remonstrance, of warning, of entreaty, of rebuke. We shall circulate unsparingly and extensively antislavery tracts and periodicals. We shall enlist the pulpit and the press in the cause of suffering and the dumb. We shall spare no exertions nor means to bring the whole nation to speedy repentance."[2] The Philadelphia convention evoked hostility but, also, growing support. Lovejoy headed the local group formed in Madison County. Beecher suggested that the call for the Illinois convention should not stress slavery as the issue but rather the right to discuss slavery. However, Lovejoy felt that Beecher attempted to draw fine distinctions that would make no great difference; no one would rally to the cause of a free press who did not also believe in

freedom for human beings. Back on July 6, Lovejoy had editorialized: "Is it not time that [an Illinois state antislavery
society] be formed? There are many . . . friends of the cause in
this state and their number is daily increasing. Ought not
measures be taken to embody their influence [for] . . . the holy
cause of emancipation?"[3]

On August 15, 1837, the call went out under Lovejoy's name
for a state antislavery convention to be held in Alton on October
26. Freedom of the press would be discussed also, since the
meeting would be in Alton. Lovejoy specifically directed that the
meeting should enlist the "friends of free enquiry." There were
255 names signed to the call for the convention. Signing were
"fifty-six gentlemen of Quincy; forty-two of Galesburg; thirty-
two of Jacksonville; twenty-three of the Altons [Alton, Middletown, and Upper Alton were then separate municipalities];
twenty of Springfield; and seventy-two in other places."[4] Significantly, no one south of Alton signed the convention call. Two
weeks after the call went out, Lovejoy wrote to a wealthy New
York supporter of the antislavery cause, "It is very desirable you
should be here two, or at least one week, before the meeting that
we might have your counsel."[5] The New Yorker did not make it,
but Lovejoy tried every realistic possibility that might boost his
cause.

Beecher felt that by limiting the meeting to those who were
opposed to slavery, Lovejoy had made a mistake. He made a trip
to Alton to discuss the matter and finally convinced Lovejoy that
first an attempt should be made to get all segments of the
community behind freedom of the press. From the academic
chair in Jacksonville, that seemed like the right thing to do.
Lovejoy felt it simply a waste of time or worse, a method of
further arousing his enemies.

Not in a position where he could afford to lose any more
friends, Lovejoy agreed to go along with Beecher. Beecher set a

meeting for the ministers and church officials in Alton to discuss the scheduled statewide meeting. The village president told them he felt the meeting should be "perfectly uncommitted" on the slavery issue; the big topic should be defense of the freedom of the press. Beecher urged the church leaders to be present and to get "their friends to attend." He then published a letter in the *Alton Telegraph* asking people interested in "free inquiry" to attend the statewide meeting. By letters and personal contact, he also urged "intelligent and influential men to attend" in the hope of restoring law and order to the Alton scene.[6]

Beecher tried to get the state convention of Presbyterians to pass a resolution expressing unanimous opposition "against the outrages at Alton and in favor of the right of free discussion." There was division on the question—those opposed arguing that it would violate the principle of the separation of church and state to pass such a resolution. Beecher commented: "As I was ashamed to have such resolutions pass by a divided vote, I withdrew them, though they could have been passed by a decided majority."[7] But Beecher's prominence gave an aura of respectability to Lovejoy's cause, encouraged Lovejoy, and discouraged the editor's opponents. The *Missouri Republican* commented: "We regret that the head of the Jacksonville College has become identified with the course of these fanatics. . . . Policy, and we think, propriety, should have induced the reverend gentleman to have been at least a silent spectator, rather than a busy participator."[8]

Lovejoy at this time headed the district organization of the Presbyterian Church in the Alton area, serving as moderator. This indicated that those who got to know him well had a high regard for him. (He had earlier led the presbytery in the St. Louis area.) The fact that a small number of respectable people encouraged him made him even more determined in his stand. Two weeks before he died, he wrote these words on a letter he received: "I have kept a good conscience in the matter, and that more than repays me for all I have suffered or can suffer. I have sworn eternal opposition to slavery, and, by the blessing of God, I will never go back. Amen."[9]

While the Abolitionists prepared for the meeting—confused somewhat by Beecher's letter saying the meeting was for those who favored the right to express views on slavery—the proslavery element prepared as well. They decided that the Colonization Society should be revived. The proslavery people wanted to avoid having only one meeting of respectable citizens on slavery, and they went all-out in their efforts to set up a meeting of the Colonization Society—two days before the Illinois antislavery meeting. They posted handbills around Alton for the meeting, indicating that those opposed to the policies of the *Observer* should attend. The handbills were unsigned, but people in Alton knew who supported the meeting.

They secured as their main speaker Cyrus Edwards, state senator, brother of a former Illinois governor, and himself the candidate on the Whig ticket at this time for governor of Illinois. The Edwards name had great respect. Political leaders would think twice before crossing the opinion of the man who seemed destined to become the next governor of Illinois. (He ended up losing by a narrow 926 votes.) Edwards had been a member of the Colonization movement for some years, even at the time when it had been unpopular. Times had changed, however, and slave owners now welcomed the movement. If free blacks could be sent to Africa, the owners felt that their slaves would be much less likely to revolt—and almost every slaveholder feared the ghost of revolt.

Another prominent speaker at the Colonization Society would be Rev. John Mason Peck, a respected Baptist minister and an opponent of Lovejoy who founded a small Baptist college in Alton, later known as Shurtleff College. The Colonization Society also listed a second minister, Rev. Joel Parker of New Orleans, as a speaker. He became well known for defending slavery as something the Bible insisted the country must follow. Parker had another badge of respectability: he visited Alton as the house guest of the wealthy Alton businessman Benjamin Godfrey, one of the men who had originally been helpful to Lovejoy. (In later years, Parker became president of Union Theological Seminary in New York City.)

The two chieftains in arranging all this were not prominently featured. They were Illinois Attorney General Usher Linder and a combination Methodist preacher-legislator-businessman, Rev. John Hogan. (After the Civil War, Hogan represented St. Louis in the U.S. House of Representatives.) Hogan and Linder had met in Vandalia, then the Illinois state capital, where they served in the state House of Representatives with a young, second-term member from Sangamon County, Abraham Lincoln.

Linder, new as attorney general, had just been elected by the Illinois General Assembly. Tall and awkward, like Lincoln, he happened to come originally from the same section of Kentucky as the future president. Lincoln dressed poorly; Linder dressed like a New York banker. Linder had a reputation as a clever and powerful speaker, but crude in language and not able to control his drinking habits. In Vandalia, when the legislature met, he stayed in a private home with an Illinois judge, Theophilus Smith, who had been indicted and was one of the least desirable influences on early Illinois politics. Linder had more than his share of bad habits, but he had political ambition and felt that riding public sentiment against the Abolitionists and against Lovejoy would help his political future. Only twenty-eight years old, he appeared to have a bright political future, and no one knew that better than Linder himself. Rev. John Hogan, the other legislator who helped arrange the Colonization meeting, was also politically ambitious but not vicious as Linder. Hogan, short and red-faced, a talkative man, made friends easily. Born in Ireland, he spoke with a distinct Irish brogue.

Linder and Hogan were the two most prominent public officials in Alton, and most of the prominent people in the area were associated with their meeting. The only big name they could not include was that of Robert Smith, local legislator and political leader who later became an influential member of Congress. Smith typified too many. As his biographer notes, he did not participate in any of "the disgraceful acts of the mob"; by "maintaining a course of masterly inactivity he avoided giving offense and came out of the troubles with prestige unimpaired."[10] (In fact, most of the right-minded people who could have provided leadership tried to maintain "statesmanlike" positions of neutrality rather than standing up for the law.) Nevertheless, even without Smith, the Linder and Hogan meeting for Colonization emerged as a big success. Edwards and the other speakers denounced the "fanatics" with brilliant oratory. The crowd loved it, and the people of Alton loved it. One of the resolutions "cordially adopted" called on Lovejoy to "discontinue his incendiary publications."[11] Linder and Hogan were encouraged.

Meanwhile, tensions in the city mounted. Between the Colonization meeting and the Beecher/Lovejoy assembly, the *Alton Telegraph* printed an editorial, "Lesson to Rioters," pointing out that in Nashville, Tennessee, an Illinois citizen, Amos Moddy, had been awarded two thousand dollars in damages for being falsely accused of being an Abolitionist.[12] The editorial suggested that there could be economic consequences to rioters. Adding to the fears and tension in Alton was a widely circulated rumor that the Upper Alton Presbyterian Church, which Lovejoy served as pastor, had been turned into a storehouse for weapons and ammunition. That the rumor had no basis in fact did not seem to diminish its circulation.

While pressure against Lovejoy mounted in Alton, around the

nation he picked up more and more support, bolstering his determination. In Lynn, Massachusetts, the Methodists of five New England states met and adopted a resolution urging "the friends of humanity throughout the country to afford Mr. Lovejoy their support." After the adoption of the resolution, the local newspaper reported: "It was moved and carried that the Convention immediately join in prayer for that devoted servant of God, and the friends of the slave in Illinois. The President [of the convention] called on the Rev. A. D. Merrill of Andover, Mass., to lead in prayer. The spectacle presented at that moment . . . was interesting beyond description. There was a congregation of nearly a thousand Christians prostrated in solemn prayer, for a distant persecuted brother, in another church, and whose face perhaps not one in that great assembly had ever seen."[13] The *Emancipator* increasingly had words of encouragement, and Lovejoy sent a letter of thanks to the publication, concluding with words of greater hope than realism: "Illinois soon will be abolitionized."[14]

Forty-eight hours after the Colonizers met, the Illinois Antislavery Congress officially opened its meeting. People from other sections of Illinois, mostly the northern cities, particularly friends from Quincy, Galesburg, and Jacksonville, came into Alton. Most of them were either Presbyterian or Congregationalist ministers. One of those attending was Rev. David Nelson, the antislavery minister whom Lovejoy credited for his conversion to Christianity. Alanson Work and George Thompson, who later spent four years in prison in Missouri for helping slaves who had escaped from that state, traveled with Nelson from Quincy. At Lovejoy's invitation, two leaders of the Ohio Antislavery Society came.

On October 26, 1837, the Illinois Antislavery Congress met in the Presbyterian church in Upper Alton. When the antislavery forces started to gather in the church, they were astounded at whom they saw there—the leaders of the enemies of Lovejoy, including Linder and Hogan. These men had all taken advantage of Beecher's letter and general invitation, which said the meeting would be open to all interested in "free inquiry," not just to the antislavery forces. Lovejoy's fears that the Beecher invitations would be abused turned out to be correct, but it was too late to do anything about it. The meeting had to go on.

At two o'clock on this pleasant fall day, Lovejoy called the meeting to order. He appointed the well-known and elderly scholar Dr. Gideon Blackburn as the temporary chairman. Lovejoy then named an Alton man, one of his strong supporters, Amherst graduate Rev. Frederick W. Graves, as temporary secretary. Those there—supposedly to defend the right of freedom of speech—vigorously opposed the Graves appointment. Confusion and shouting followed. Many of Lovejoy's supporters, including Winthrop Gilman, were not present. Also absent when the meeting started was Beecher, but not long after the meeting began, Beecher walked in. He had stopped overnight in Carlinville on his way to Alton from Jacksonville, and while in Carlinville, he had heard there might be trouble at the meeting. Beecher describes what happened:

> I entered the house in which the convention was assembled and found a tumultuous speaker claiming seats for himself and his friends. None of those citizens of Alton on whom I had mainly relied to unite good men and sustain the law were there. I was also informed that some of those claiming seats had already shown their views on freedom of the press; they were responsible for the destruction of the press of the *Observer*.
>
> Lovejoy soon informed me that they were claiming seats on the basis of my notice in the Alton *Telegraph*. Lovejoy had objected to the admission because they had come in to interrupt the meeting and not to maintain the cause of a free press. At this they were highly indignant.[15]

Beecher then suggested that first only those who believed in freedom for the slaves should be permitted to vote and participate; if that group wanted to expand it to others who claimed to be interested in a free press and the right of free discussion, they should be admitted also. Immediately one of Lovejoy's bitterest opponents said that he felt all of those present could agree on the basic principles; they intended to stay and participate. After much shouting, with charges and countercharges, the chairman finally adjourned the meeting until nine o'clock the next morning. The minutes of the meeting noted simply: "In consequence of . . . a number of disorderly persons, the convention did not duly organize during the afternoon."[16]

After this meeting broke up, Attorney General Linder gathered his friends and some curious citizens around a woodpile at the side of the church. Linder used his great oratorical abilities to blast the Abolitionists. The Abolitionists complained about losing their right to freedom of speech and yet they tried to deny that same right to those who disagreed, Linder told the group assembled outside the church. In colorful language, he denounced Lovejoy and all the antislavery forces. Carried away with his speaking abilities, he also condemned the temperance societies that Lovejoy supported. Someone shouted to the heavy-drinking Linder that after one of his recent drinking sprees, Linder had joined a temperance society. The group laughed, temporarily embarrassing Linder, but he recovered quickly to change the subject to Abolitionists. His final word to his friends gathered around him was that they should all be present the next morning.

That Thursday night after the meeting, Lovejoy and the antislavery leaders met privately and discussed what to do. They finally decided that the original letter calling for the convention would be read. Anyone who favored the immediate freeing of the slaves and freedom of the press could vote or participate. This ought to make it clear who could take part, they thought.

Dr. Blackburn opened the meeting at nine o'clock on Friday, October 27. The chairman explained that only those who believed in the purposes of the convention could participate. The anti-Lovejoy forces said they were in full agreement and would take part in the convention. Obviously, they were not sincere. Lovejoy and his friends had miscalculated badly. Not honoring the sacredness of freedom, property, and life, these men would not honor the sacredness of truth.

Then, another disturbing event happened. The trustees of the church, which Lovejoy served as pastor, had been frightened into passing a resolution stating that the church could not be used unless all who wanted to participate could do so. The church resolution—plus the decision of the previous night to admit anyone who agreed to the principles of the convention—meant that Lovejoy and the Antislavery Society had to go ahead with their enemies outnumbering them. Among those present were the four who would later claim credit for killing Lovejoy.

On the first order of business, the election of officers, Dr. Blackburn became one candidate. The other, a local physician, Dr. Thomas Hope, had been plotting against Lovejoy and would share the guilt for his death in less than two weeks. The group elected Blackburn by a vote of 73–53. Then, they elected two secretaries. By the time of the election of the second secretary, enough of the anti-Lovejoy forces had walked into the morning meeting that the election of the second secretary went to William Carr, one of the crudest of those who fought Lovejoy. After the election of officers, the chairman, Dr. Blackburn, named a committee of three to draw up resolutions that would be debated in the afternoon. He named to the committee Linder, Beecher, and a minister who was known for being sympathetic to Lovejoy, thus giving the pro-Lovejoy forces two of the three members.

To no one's surprise, the committee could not agree. During its meeting, Beecher asked Linder how the day before he could favor freedom of the press and the immediate freeing of the slaves and be against them the next day. Linder answered simply that if he could agree yesterday, he couldn't today. The two in the majority on the committee submitted portions of the Illinois constitution for adoption. They figured that Linder, the attorney general of Illinois, could hardly disagree with the constitution that he had sworn to uphold. But he did disagree. Getting ahead politically was his objective. In the afternoon, two reports were given, one by Beecher for the two-person majority and one by Linder for himself in the minority. Linder's was an all-out proslavery resolution calling slaves property and saying the constitution prohibits taking away a person's property. At one point during the meeting, Linder got excited in his oratory and "shook his fist insultingly in the face of Lovejoy, within about two feet of him."[17] People crowded the afternoon meeting and, after much debate, adopted the proslavery resolutions, and the convention dissolved. The proslavery forces scored a clear victory; they had made the whole purpose of the convention meaningless.

Lovejoy's friends were afraid to meet together that night, so they gathered in private homes for prayer and discussion. The next night, Saturday, October 28, about thirty of Lovejoy's friends—one report says fifty-five—met in the home of Rev. Thaddeus Hurlbut, to discuss what to do. One of those at the meeting, Enoch Long, a businessman and a veteran of the War of 1812, arranged to have himself deputized as a constable. He in turn deputized a number of friends he could count on. Long recalled later that he had recruited and deputized forty men. When ruffians threatened to come into Hurlbut's home and break up the meeting, Long and his friends quickly chased them away. (Long did not become as prominent in the Lovejoy struggle as his business associate, Winthrop Gilman, but he had a closer social relationship with Lovejoy; the Long and Lovejoy families visited together frequently.)

Only once did people threaten to attack the Hurlbut home. The rest of the time, Lovejoy's friends had a quiet, orderly meeting, trying to decide the best course for the Alton *Observer* and for opponents of slavery. The small group voted to encourage Lovejoy to continue publishing the *Observer* in Alton. They also voted to start the Illinois Antislavery Society. The *Missouri Republican* account reads: "On Saturday about thirty of the Abolitionists congregated together in a private house in Upper Alton, where having locked themselves up, they proceeded to form a State Anti-Slavery Society."[18] Otherwise it was a quiet day.

Sunday afternoon, October 29, the small Presbyterian church that Lovejoy served as pastor had Beecher as its guest speaker. The crowded congregation seemed impressed by what Beecher said on the subject of slavery. Many wanted him to speak again, and the next night, Monday, October 30, he spoke once more in the same church. Gilman invited Mayor Krum to attend, and he did. When those attending the church emerged, some boys and a smaller number of adults taunted those coming out of the church, some of whom were armed. The mayor immediately stepped forward and urged everyone to go home, which they did. That same day, the *Missouri Republican* came out with an editorial expressing regret that Alton, "this young city, has been made the theatre of the operations of these fanatics." The editorial added: "We are well assured that the mass, the bone and sinew of the community, are totally opposed to the agitation of the subject" of slavery.[19] This was eight days before Lovejoy's death.

Tuesday afternoon, October 31, one week before Lovejoy expected a new press, Gilman went with Lovejoy to see the mayor. They told the mayor that the new press would be arriving soon and that they wanted authority to be officially organized to defend the press if defense would be needed. The group might also have to defend meetings. The mayor quickly agreed and told them he would cooperate fully. Lovejoy tried to persuade Mayor

Krum to head the semi-organized defense force they were going to form, but the mayor declined.

That night, the Colonization Society met and again had a distinguished list of speakers. Cyrus Edwards spoke once more, and when he finished, the *Alton Telegraph* reported, there was "cheering from every part of the house."[20] But the Colonization Society meeting developed nothing new except to underscore once again that most of the respected people in the community were not on Lovejoy's side.

Wednesday evening, November 1, Beecher spoke on slavery in the larger and older First Presbyterian Church. Tension was mounting in Alton, and the public, sensing excitement, filled every corner in the church. The mayor came. Beecher had achieved polish and effectiveness as a speaker, and the audience listened with quiet intensity to every word. The dramatic stillness in the church was broken only by Beecher's carefully chosen words until a stone came hurling through the window with a loud crash. A man in the balcony shouted: "To arms!" Hidden in a house next to the church, the protective police Gilman and Lovejoy had organized came out immediately when they heard the crash from the rock and the shout from the balcony. Fully armed, they quickly frightened away the troublemakers, and the meeting in the church continued undisturbed while the armed men stood on guard outside. When the people in the church came out after the program had ended, some boys gathered outside once again and shouted at them, but no violence occurred. Late that night, a few men, perhaps drunks, came to the Lovejoy home shouting threats. Lovejoy appeared at the door with a gun, and they disappeared quickly. That day, the *Missouri Republican* commented: "If these fanatics will persist . . . the already outraged community will [cause] a result to be regretted by all."[21]

Thursday, November 2, the entire community knew that another press soon would arrive in the face of public opinion mounting in intensity against Lovejoy. Even Rev. John Hogan, who with Linder had arranged the Colonization meetings, feared that public opinion had reached "a terrible state of things."[22] On Wednesday, he had met Beecher and Gilman on the street, commented on what he feared might happen, and agreed to arrange a meeting for the next day at his store, a meeting of leading citizens to try to reach a compromise and quiet tempers in the city. Beecher thought it a good idea, and so on Thursday afternoon, a group gathered. It quickly became apparent that most of the people who gathered for the meeting at the Hogan store were not friends of Lovejoy.

Hogan opened the meeting by saying that the purpose was to find a compromise that would halt "the present excited state of public sentiment." He said he hoped for the "restoration of harmony and good fellowship" through some kind of compromise. Beecher then presented a nine-point resolution beginning with the assurance that "every citizen may freely speak, write and print on any subject."[23] Beecher's resolution affirmed Lovejoy's right to express his opinions, however unpopular, as well as the duty of the public and its officials to protect his freedom to do so. Gilman joined Beecher in offering the resolution, but those present did not want to hear that kind of resolution. Beecher quoted from Daniel Webster and from newspapers in slave states. He attempted no defense of Lovejoy's opinions but simply said that Lovejoy had a right to hold any opinions, whether right or wrong.

Attorney General Linder rose to respond to Beecher and could find nothing good in the resolutions. Beecher later noted: "I had before me not an infuriated mob, but those who gloried in being thought of as the calm, thoughtful and judicious men of the area." Beecher said he felt a chill "when not a single voice was raised in behalf of principles so sound."[24] The group appointed a seven-member committee to consider the resolutions, but of the seven members, only Gilman supported Lovejoy. (Lovejoy himself did not attend.) The meeting adjourned until two o'clock the next afternoon, Friday. However, that Thursday night the Colonization Society had another meeting, with Hogan and two others as speakers, all of them bitter in their denunciation of Abolitionists in general and Lovejoy and the *Observer* in particular.

On Friday, November 3, four days before Lovejoy's death, Beecher, feeling extremely depressed from the meeting the day before, stayed in his room and prayed. Lovejoy interrupted him once, joined him in a prayer, and then left. Beecher recalled Lovejoy's visit that morning: "Never shall I forget the calmness of Mr. Lovejoy's mind, his sense of the presence of God, the childlike confidence with which he committed his cause to Him that heareth prayer. How he prayed especially for the best good of the community in which he dwelt! He earnestly asked God for strength that he might not betray his own cause in the hour of trial. He was perfectly cool and collected."[25]

Friday afternoon, the same Lovejoy supporters and opponents assembled; Lovejoy attended this meeting. Outside the hall near the Riley Building, a man named Arthur Jourdon stood, stopping Lovejoy's foes who walked by and urging them to join the meeting. After the presiding officer called the assemblage to order, Linder offered a resolution to quiet the most effective person Lovejoy's side had—Beecher. The resolution said that the meeting should be composed "exclusively of the citizens of Madison County; and that it is requested that none others shall vote or take part in the discussions of any subject that may be offered."[26] They adopted the resolution unanimously. Lovejoy's friends were so outnumbered they did not even put up a struggle. Now their most effective voice had been silenced.

Then the seven-person committee reported, the committee that had been designated to consider the resolutions proposed by Beecher calling for freedom of the press. They rejected the Beecher resolutions and introduced substitute resolutions asking

Lovejoy to sever his connections with the *Observer* and to leave Alton. To soften the blow, they called this necessary in the interest of "peace and harmony" and said that the resolution did not intend to reflect "in the slightest degree upon the private character or motives" of Lovejoy. Cyrus Edwards, state senator and Whig candidate for governor, made the report for the committee. Edwards defended the resolution by citing the tension in the community: "It is not to be disguised, that parties are now organizing and arming for a conflict, which may terminate in a train of mournful consequences."[27] Gilman immediately protested and said the group should simply support law and order and the freedoms of all citizens.

When Gilman finished speaking, Lovejoy arose. He slowly walked to the front of the room, put his coat aside and quietly started to speak. His words are among the most moving and courageous in defense of free speech:

It is proper that I should state the whole matter as I understand it, before this audience. I do not stand here to argue the question as presented by the report of the committee. My only wonder is that . . . the chairman of that committee — for whose character I entertain great respect, though I have not had the pleasure of getting personally acquainted . . . could have brought himself to submit such a report.

Mr. Chairman, I do not admit that it is the business of this assembly to decide whether I shall or shall not publish a newspaper in this city. The gentlemen have, as the lawyers say, made a wrong issue. I have the right to do it. I know that I have the right freely to speak and publish my sentiments, subject only to the laws of the land for the abuse of that right. This right was given me by my Maker, and is solemnly guaranteed to me by the constitution of these United States and of this state.

What I wish to know of you is whether you will protect me in the exercise of this right; or whether . . . I am to continue to be subjected to personal indignity and outrage.

These resolutions . . . are spoken of as a compromise—a compromise between two parties. Mr. Chairman, this is not so. There is but one party here. It is simply a question of whether the law shall be enforced, or whether the mob shall be allowed . . . to continue to trample under their feet . . . the rights of an innocent individual.

Mr. Chairman, what have I to compromise? If freely to forgive those who have so greatly injured me, if to pray for their temporal and eternal happiness, if still to wish for the prosperity of your city and state—notwithstanding all the indignities I have suffered in it— if this be the compromise intended, then do I willingly make it. My rights have been shamefully, wickedly outraged; this I know, and feel, and can never forget. But I can and do freely forgive those who have done it.

But if by a compromise is meant that I should cease from doing that which duty requires of me, I cannot make it. And the reason is that I fear God more than I fear man. Think not that I would lightly go contrary to public sentiment around me. The good opinion of my fellow men is dear to me, and I would sacrifice anything but principle to obtain their good wishes; but when they ask me to surrender this, they ask for more than I can—[more] than I dare give. . . .

God, in his providence—so say all my brethren, and so I think— has devolved upon me the responsibility of maintaining my ground here; and, Mr. Chairman, I am determined to do it. A voice comes to me from Maine, from Massachusetts, from Connecticut, from New York, from Pennsylvania—yea, from Kentucky, from Mississippi, from Missouri—calling upon me in the name of all that is dear in heaven or earth, to stand fast; and by the help of God, I will stand. I know I am but one and you are many. My strength would avail but little against you all. You can crush me if you will; but I shall die at my post, for I cannot and will not forsake it.

Why should I flee from Alton? Is this not a free state? When attacked by a mob at St. Louis, I came here to be at the home of freedom and of the laws. The mob has pursued me here, and why should I retreat again? Where can I be safe if not here? Have I not a right to claim the protection of the laws? Sir, the very act of retreating will embolden the mob to follow me wherever I go. No sir, there is no way to escape the mob, but to abandon the path of duty. And that, God helping me, I will never do.

It has been said here, that my hand is against every man, and every man's hand against me. The last part of the declaration is too painfully true. I do indeed find almost every man's hand against me, but against whom in this place has my hand been raised? I appeal to every individual present. Whom of you have I injured? Whose character have I traduced? Whose family have I molested? Whose business have I meddled with? If any, let him rise here and testify against me.

[No one answers.]

. . . If in anything I have offended against the law, I am not so popular in this community that it would be difficult to convict me. You have courts and judges and juries; they find nothing against me. And now you come together for the purpose of driving out a confessedly innocent man, for no cause but that he dares to think and speak as his conscience and his God dictate. Will conduct like this stand the scrutiny of your country? Of posterity?

Pause, I beseech you, and reflect. The present excitement will soon be over. The voice of conscience will at last be heard. [The time will come] as you review the scenes of this hour, [that] you will be forced to say: "He was right. He was right."

But you have been exhorted, in driving me away to affix no unnecessary disgrace upon me. Sir, I reject all such compassion. You cannot disgrace me. Scandal and falsehood and calumny have already done their worst. My shoulders have borne burden until it sits easy upon them. You may hang me . . . as the mob hung up the individuals of Vicksburg. You may burn me at the stake, as they did McIntosh at St. Louis; or you may tar and feather me, or throw me into the Mississippi, as you have often threatened to do; but you cannot disgrace me.

I—and I alone—can disgrace myself; and the deepest of all disgrace would be at a time like this to deny my Master by forsaking His cause. He died for me; and I were most unworthy to bear His name, should I refuse, if need be, to die for Him.

You have been told that I have a family who are dependent on me. And this has been given as a reason why I should be driven off as gently as possible. It is true, Mr. Chairman, that I am a husband and father. And this it is that adds the bitterest ingredient to the cup of sorrow I am called to drink. I am made to feel the wisdom of the

Apostle's advice: "It is better not to marry." I know, sir, that in this contest I stake not only my life but that of others also. I do not expect my wife will ever recover from the shock she received at the scenes through which she was called to pass at St. Charles. And how was it the other night, on my return to my house? I found her driven to the garret, through fear of the mob who were prowling round my house. And scarcely had I entered the house ere my windows were broken in by brickbats from the mob. And she [was] so alarmed that it was impossible for her to sleep or rest that night.

I am hunted like as a partridge upon the mountains. I am pursued as a felon through your streets. And to the guardian power of the law I look in vain for that protection against violence which even the vilest criminal may claim.

Yet think not that I am unhappy. Think not that I regret the choice that I have made. While all around me is violence and tumult, all is peace within. An approving conscience and the rewarding smile of God is a full recompense for all that I forego and all that I endure. Yes, sir, I enjoy a peace which nothing can destroy. I sleep sweetly and undisturbed, except when awakened by the brickbats of the mob.

No, sir, I am not unhappy. I have counted the cost, and stand prepared freely to offer up my all in the service of God. Yes, sir, I am fully aware of all the sacrifice I make in here pledging myself to continue this contest to the last.

[A moment of silence.]

Forgive these tears—I had not intended to shed them. And they flow not for myself, but others. But I am commanded to forsake father and mother and wife and children for Jesus' sake; and as His professed disciple I stand prepared to do it. The time for fulfilling this pledge in my case, it seems to me, has come.

Sir, I dare not flee away from Alton. Should I attempt it, I should feel that the angel of the Lord with his flaming sword was pursuing me wherever I went. It is because I fear God that I am not afraid of all who oppose me in this city. No, sir, the contest has commenced here; and here it must be finished. Before God and you all, I here pledge myself to continue it—if need be, till death. If I fall, my grave shall be made in Alton.[28]

Lovejoy left the hall after speaking. Even some of his bitter enemies were crying when Lovejoy finished. Beecher put his head on his knees and cried uncontrollably. He wrote later that never in his life had he been so overcome by emotions.

If at that moment one of the opponents had publicly switched sides, perhaps history would have been different. One young man present, Dr. Benjamin K. Hart, said he "was on the point of rising to say something that would help the turn of the tide. But I was young then, and, as you know, have always been rather deficient in self-confidence. So I hesitated—and hesitated a moment too long." He added: "I have never forgiven myself for my hesitation."[29]

Instead, the popular Hogan spoke next. He pointed out that the apostle Paul, being threatened with death in Damascus, did not defy the people but had himself let down on the outside of the city wall in a basket and escaped. Lovejoy, he said, should follow the example of the apostle Paul and not his own warped thinking. Hogan urged Lovejoy "to abstain from the exercise of some of his abstract rights." Hogan added that Lovejoy had broken his pledge, that he had come to Alton with the understanding that he would write less about slavery than he did in St. Louis. At this point, Rev. F. W. Graves, one of Lovejoy's supporters, rose and asked Hogan in front of the group: "Didn't the editor of the *Observer* tell that first meeting that he would give up none of his right to discuss any subject which he saw fit?" Hogan admitted that to be correct.[30]

Attorney General Linder then rose and asked "whether the interest and feelings of the citizens of Alton should be consulted or whether we are to be dictated to by foreigners [i.e., Lovejoy and Beecher]. . . ." He also hinted that Lovejoy was insane. Beecher called Linder's speech "unequaled by anything I ever heard for an excited, bitter, vindictive spirit." After his vicious but effective speech, Linder introduced a resolution "that the discussion of the doctrines of immediate abolitionism, as they have been discussed in the columns of the Alton *Observer*, would be destructive of the peace and harmony of the citizens of Alton, and that, therefore, we cannot recommend the reestablishment of that paper."[31] After much discussion of the resolution, the group assembled accepted it.

Shortly before the meeting adjourned, the mayor, trying to keep peace with all sides, offered a resolution stating that the group favored "order, peace and constitutional law" but expressed "regret that persons and editors from abroad have seen proper to interest themselves so conspicuously in the discussion and agitation" of the slavery question. They adopted this resolution also, and then the meeting ended. Before the final gavel sounded, Lovejoy had been labeled wicked, deluded, and insane. At one point, someone proposed a resolution that the group should support the mayor in the suppression of violence. They defeated that resolution.

Word about the afternoon meeting spread quickly Friday night. People learned that Lovejoy would not leave under any circumstances and that the leading city and state officials did not seem to frown on violence. Linder told one person after the meeting, "Elijah Lovejoy will be killed within two weeks."[32]

At home early that evening, Lovejoy talked with his sister, who had come from Maine to visit with her brothers. Suddenly, a large brick shattered the living room window, coming through the window at a speed that could have meant death. It narrowly missed both Lovejoy and his sister. During the day, the *Missouri Republican*, which circulated widely in Alton, reported that Lovejoy "was to receive another press in a few days."[33] During these days of crisis, Beecher found Lovejoy calm: "I never saw him when he did not have his feelings under complete control. And I have known him intimately in the scenes of his deepest trial. Never did I hear him, even in his most unguarded hours, utter an angry, an impatient, or a vindictive word. During the days which he spent at my house a few weeks before his death, we were all struck with his uncommonly mild and gentle frame of mind. Never did I know a man who had so keen a relish for the joys of home. His inexpressible love for his son I shall never forget. Perhaps even then he thought that his son might soon be deprived of a father's care."[34]

ᐱ 7

ᐱ Death

Sunday morning, November 5, 1837, was the last time mob members and their opponents listened quietly while someone else spoke. The men who would defend the new press and the men who would murder Lovejoy sat side by side singing hymns.

Sunday and Monday, word reached Lovejoy's friends and his enemies that the new press was aboard the *Missouri Fulton*, docked in St. Louis. Mayor Krum again met with Gilman and Lovejoy at the three-year-old hotel known as the Mansion House and agreed to allow the formation of a militia to defend the press. Gilman assured the mayor that the loosely organized military group would "at all times hold themselves in readiness to obey any command" from the mayor.[1] Gilman and Lovejoy asked the mayor to appoint someone to be in charge, and the mayor named William Harned but later withdrew the appointment, saying he had no authority to make such a move.

Where to place the press posed the next problem. At first, arrangements were made to put it in the Roff hardware store, but Gilman and the others decided that would be a difficult position to defend. Gilman suggested that the press be placed in the warehouse that he and Godfrey owned, a stone building separated from the river only by a wharf and a street. It was the largest warehouse on the riverfront. That took courage for Gilman, for the warehouse contained the city's largest merchandise collection.

They planned to move the press quickly from the boat, across the street, and into the stone warehouse. Built on a hill that sloped down to the river, the building appeared three stories tall on the river side and two stories on the hill side. The bottom floor entrance on the side that faced the river made it easy to bring in a heavy press relatively quickly. Really two buildings combined, the structure measured about a hundred feet in length and forty to fifty feet in width.

On Monday, officers of the *Missouri Fulton* learned that Gilman and Lovejoy's other friends did not want the press until three o'clock Tuesday morning. Gilman figured that at that hour there would be much less chance for hostile action against the press. Monday night, the Alton City Council met. According to the City Council minutes, Mayor Krum told the council that "individual citizens" had come to him believing that their property would be in danger, asking for the appointment of special constables to defend the property. The mayor's report also stated "that they believed themselves to be insecure in their persons." The mayor asked city council approval of the request with the statement that he "had much reason to believe that the peace of the city would be disturbed." After the mayor's presentation, one of the aldermen suggested a resolution that the mayor and the city council "address a note to Mr. Lovejoy and his friends, requesting them to relinquish the idea of establishing an Abolition press at this time in the city." The city council ended without taking action on either request, and word of this quickly spread around the city.

Both Sunday night and Monday night, a group of ten to fifteen men armed with pistols and clubs watched along the riverfront for the Missouri Fulton to arrive. They intended to throw the press into the river quickly. Monday night, they broke up the wait with occasional trips to a nearby tavern, but the combination of drinking and waiting for a second night was too much. Late that night, they went home.

Monday evening, about thirty of Lovejoy's followers met at Gilman's store to organize themselves into a voluntary company to protect the property and the press. They picked Enoch Long, the only one among them with military experience, as their captain. They planned to spend the night in Gilman's warehouse, and they armed themselves. One of them, a young lawyer, Massachusetts-born John Chickering, borrowed a gun from his law partner, who laughed when he handed it to Chickering, assuring him that there would be no need to use it.

Close to three o'clock in the morning, Gilman spotted the *Missouri Fulton* approaching Alton. He and a companion went to Mayor Krum's home and awakened him, asking him to come to the wharf to suppress any violence should it arise. Krum immediately dressed and joined them, as on the previous afternoon he had promised Gilman and Lovejoy he would. The armed men remained in the stone warehouse as the boat landed. They stationed themselves at "commanding points" in the warehouse so that any hostile action would be met with gunfire before anyone could get near the press.

Gilman and the mayor walked down to the boat and watched while the boat's crew moved the crated press toward the building. As they moved the press, a horn suddenly sounded in the city, probably a prearranged signal to those bent on violence that the press had arrived, but at that hour, the signal went unnoticed by the sleeping citizens. Lovejoy's friends moved the press into the building with surprising ease and quiet.

Lovejoy did not go to the warehouse while all this happened. He stayed at his home, ready to defend his house from the frequent attacks made on it and comforting his expectant wife who was under great emotional strain. Shortly after Lovejoy expected the press to arrive, he went into the room in his home where Beecher was sleeping and awakened him. The two dressed quickly and walked through the dark Alton streets toward the river to see whether there had been violence. Beecher recalled that the streets were "empty and silent, and the sounds of our feet echoed from the walls as we passed along."[2]

The silence was, of course, a good sign. They reached the warehouse with the boat still moored nearby, while the boat's crew and volunteer guards were lifting the heavy press to the third floor. Lovejoy and Beecher helped them. A happy group looked at the press admiringly after it had been put in place. There had been no mob and no fight. A horn had sounded, but no one responded. The crisis appeared to be over. The big stone warehouse seemed a safe fortress from any attack. Lovejoy's group decided that the total number of volunteers could be divided into small groups of six for each successive night, and for the little time that remained of this night, Lovejoy and Beecher volunteered to stand guard. (The mayor had suggested that the press should be guarded.)

In minutes rather than hours, the sun came up, and the scene Lovejoy and Beecher saw inspired them: a great river next to which a great fight for freedom appeared to have been won. Beecher crawled onto the roof to view the scene of the bright red sun rising over the river and the countryside. He felt that nature had never looked more beautiful and that "a bloodless battle had been gained for God and for the truth; and that Alton was redeemed from eternal shame."[3] Soon the sounds of business activity filled the morning air, and Lovejoy and Beecher felt free to return to Lovejoy's home. The fight seemed to be over. The press appeared to be safe, and Beecher decided after consultation with Lovejoy to return to Illinois College in Jacksonville. Before Beecher departed, he and Lovejoy went into the room where Celia Ann lay ill. The three had a final word of prayer together — much more final than any of them knew. As Beecher left, he told Lovejoy's wife that the "days of trial were nearly over and that more peaceful hours were soon coming."[4] Beecher then left the quiet home. On his way out of town, he heard rumors of an attack on the warehouse, but he dismissed them as another of many tales that plagued the local scene.

During the day on Tuesday, word spread quickly that the press had landed. "The excitement became intense," one citizen recalled. "The only topic of conversation was Lovejoy's press."[5] In the taverns, talk got rougher and rougher, and Lovejoy's friends were now genuinely frightened. Gilman took his wife and infant child out of town, and Lovejoy sent his wife and son to another home near the church that he served as minister.

A spectator at the climactic event later recalled: "There was an element in favor of destroying it [the press] at all hazards, even if it took his [Lovejoy's] life. This was common talk on the streets. While this element was composed largely of the rougher class of people, I could give the names of ministers of the gospel who were encouraging the destruction of the press, when by a few words these same influential men could have settled the matter in Lovejoy's favor."[6]

Before the sun went down, a temporary military company officially formed at Gilman's urging, a mixture of many interested individuals, including some young men, apparently only interested in a little excitement. It soon became apparent that they would have more excitement than they wanted. Forty-two signed the roster for membership in the company, but only fourteen were willing to stay and defend the building that night. The forty-two men stood in a circle when the call came for volunteers. Those who volunteered stepped forward. One man, Joseph Greeley, later related his experience: "I was told that an Independent Militia company was to be formed that evening [and] . . . that the individuals favorable to the formation . . . were to meet at Godfrey and Gilman's store that evening. . . . I declined going on the ground that I feared it might be an abolition meeting, but was assured that it was no such thing. . . . They requested me to sign a paper. . . . The number of people which the law requires having signed the paper, we proceeded to an election of officers. . . . After we had made [the] choice of officers we proceeded up into the second story where we found some arms. We took them and paraded and drilled for a little time, but as the guns were loaded we did not exercise much. This was between seven and eight in the evening. About eight o'clock the inquiry was made, 'Who would stay and defend the building that night?' The company were at this time in a circle, and some of them stepped forward and volunteered. I was asked to stay, but declined doing so, and went home."[7] Several others who did not volunteer were asked privately whether they would stay, but they declined. Gilman and his friends had thirty or forty weapons available, mostly guns borrowed from Roff's store. While most of those who volunteered understood the seriousness of the endeavor, a few apparently volunteered "to have some crackers and cheese, and to hear some good stories."[8]

The warehouse building that housed Lovejoy's press was one block long; it had doors and windows at each end but no windows on the other two sides. The roofs were made of wood—a fact that soon would become important. The lack of windows on two sides could enable a small group to defend the building against gunfire, but it also meant that action taken by any enemy at the windowless sides of the building could not be observed.

Early that evening, Gilman and a friend went to Mayor Krum, told him they feared mob action, and informed him of their preparations for possible fighting if necessary. The mayor said he believed an attack would not be made, although he did admit that people "seemed to shun me, and were very reluctant to talk with me at all." He told Gilman that the men had a right to arm themselves and that they "would be justified in defending their property" if necessary. The mayor said that if he could help in suppressing any riot, he would be available.

That same evening, about eight o'clock, Henry West stood in the doorway of his small store when a friend walked past and said there would be action that night, that preparations were underway to burn the warehouse or blow it up unless Lovejoy surrendered the press. The man urged West to go and tell Gilman. West went quickly to the warehouse and asked for Gilman. "He's upstairs," West was told. "Tell him I want to see him," West replied with a tone of urgency. "It's important." West then told Gilman the rumors around town. Gilman replied: "I have thought this matter over seriously. I will not give up the press. If necessary, I will defend this property at the risk of my life."

Excited, West did not know what to do. While West was talking to Gilman, stones were hurled at the building and someone fired a shot at the building. West quickly went back to his store but then decided to return to the warehouse. On his way to the warehouse, he met Dr. Horace Beal. West asked Dr. Beal to use his influence to stop the crowd and get them to disperse. Dr. Beal declined, saying he would have nothing to do with dispersing men willing to destroy the Abolitionist press. West returned to the warehouse with Mayor Krum and another man, Sherman Robbins, and went upstairs. While West and the mayor were there, a large stone hit one of the doors, and someone inside fired a shot. West advised them to shoot over the heads of the crowd, but according to West, Lovejoy replied, "We must not waste a fire." West then left.

Early that morning, Attorney General Usher F. Linder left town, giving legal business in nearby Greene County as the reason. As attorney general, he could have postponed such business easily, but he obviously preferred to be away so that no one could accuse him of being associated with mob action if it occurred. However, his prior conduct made it clear there would be no prosecution if men violated the law in acting against Lovejoy and his *Observer*.

About thirty minutes before the attackers arrived at the warehouse, Edward Keating, Linder's law partner who had an office near the warehouse, stopped to visit the defenders. "Each man whom I saw, except Gilman, had a gun," he reported. "The doors were not blockaded and I was astonished at the little preparation for defense I saw." One of the defenders, Henry Tanner, later wrote that "someone not possessed of much judgment" admitted Keating.[9] Tanner referred to him and another visitor, Henry West, as spies. At one point in the evening, a few of the defenders talked about keeping Keating and West as hostages. Keating returned later and noted that one other man in the group of defenders, John Noble, had no gun. Noble stated that he did not believe in the use of arms. He believed in the freedom of the press, and so he joined the group in their dangerous position. Keating said that he felt there would be violence. He left the warehouse and went to Mayor Krum's office. A few minutes later, another man stopped at the warehouse. Gilman advised him to get away from the entrance if he did not want to get hurt.

At one of the favorite drinking spots in Alton, called the Tontine, people gathering that Tuesday night were getting more and more irritated and surly about Lovejoy's new press that had been landed safely. The angrier they became, the more they drank—and the more they drank, the angrier they became. At the Tontine, William Carr, whom the anti-Lovejoy group had selected as a secretary at one of the "compromise" meetings the previous week, carried around a jug of whiskey, offering drinks and urging action against the press. After more drinking, they left the Tontine, formed a line—almost like a military line—and headed for the warehouse. As the small group marched toward the warehouse, their numbers grew. Some who went along were only curious; others wanted entertainment and were ready for a good fight; others were genuinely overcome with rage.

Early in the evening, only a few of them had guns. Most had

clubs or sticks, and some had stones. The cobblestone streets had just been completed, and plenty of large stones were available. Soon, about 150 shouting, stone-throwing men were at the side of the warehouse, about six or eight feet from the building. They quickly broke every window in the building. Later, the assemblage grew larger, but among the 150 to 300 gathered in this early part of the evening were most of the men who had attended the meetings the previous week, who had claimed to be "friends of free inquiry." Soon, as one observer commented, "the street was full."[10] Eventually, fifty to eighty armed men gathered among a much larger number.

As the crowd grew, Gilman—through an opening in an upper-story door—came out boldly in front of them on this clear moonlit night and asked why they had "come at such an unusual hour to create a disturbance?" Gilman added that he felt it his duty to defend his property and that he would do it with his life if he had to. Gilman repeated these words several times in the course of the evening. While Gilman spoke to the suddenly silent, unruly gathering, William Carr raised his pistol and pointed it at Gilman. Before he could fire, Gilman's friends spotted Carr's pistol and hastily pulled Gilman inside the building. Through one of the many broken windows, William Harned shouted to those who only watched to get out of the way.

At one point—testimony is conflicting on when—the mob broke open a door on the first floor facing the river, only to find barrels of sugar blocking further access. Lovejoy stayed inside the warehouse while all this took place. Because of the intense hatred for Lovejoy, the defenders believed it wiser to let Gilman, the highly respected Alton merchant, speak for the group. After Gilman talked to those outside the building, Carr shouted back that they did not want to injure Gilman or his property but that they intended to get the press and they would do it at the risk of their lives. As tensions mounted, each spokesman stated that he would prefer death to allowing the other group to have its way.

When Gilman came back into the building, a sudden barrage of stones from the newly repaired street broke against the building. Some in the mob, taking the whole affair as a big entertainment, did nothing more than blow tin horns they had secured somewhere. Reuben Gerry, one of the nineteen men inside the warehouse, spotted some large earthenware pots and crocks and started throwing them at the mob. The noise of stones hitting against the building and breaking windows, plus the noise of the horns and of the pots and crocks, made it difficult to tell what happened next. The accounts vary. Almost all agree that the first shots came from outside the building. Apparently, two or three rifle shots and a pistol shot were fired at the warehouse. While some shot and threw large stones, others rammed at one of the doors with a large log or piece of timber, trying to break it open. One shot came in response from the group in the warehouse. Gilman asked, "Who fired?" "I did," one of the men responded. Then two or three more shots were fired from outside.

In returning fire, one of Lovejoy's friends hit a man among the noisy crowd outside. The shot struck Lyman Bishop, a youthful carpenter, who had recently moved into the Alton area from Genesee County, New York. That afternoon, he had boasted that he would help get the Abolitionists. The bullet passed from his shoulder through his hip. One witness reported that Bishop fired first, but that is not certain. Maryland-born Dr. Beal, now part of the mob, examined him quickly and said he did not think it too serious. They took Bishop to the office of one of the local physicians, Dr. Hart, the only physician in Alton sympathetic to Lovejoy. One observer noted: "They took Bishop as they might have carried a hog, one by each limb."[11] On the way, the men carrying him met Mayor Krum. "Is he badly hurt?" the mayor asked. "We don't think so," they answered.

When the mayor returned to the scene of action, he found the mob had pulled back, temporarily frightened by the wounding of Bishop. Mayor Krum approached them and urged that they scatter and go home. As he spoke, the crowd around him grew larger, and although the mayor "used all the means in his power to get them to disperse," they were still determined to get the press. Someone shouted to the mayor to go into the warehouse and tell those inside that they wanted the press. They agreed that if the mayor would do that, they would retire while he negotiated.

The mayor went into the warehouse with two men, probably the same visit West had described. He told Gilman what the crowd wanted, adding that probably he could control them when he went back out. While in the warehouse, he visited with Lovejoy and the others and told them that they were justified in shooting to protect their property. One of the two men who accompanied the mayor reported that those inside seemed "firm, cool and collected." The candles that lit the rooms gave the warehouse an eerie appearance. As the mayor said, he stayed in the warehouse "some time purposely . . . in order that the excitement should subside, as I had no doubt it would."[12] But those outside did not go home; they continued drinking. And word of the excitement, plus the noise, attracted more people.

One man, Solomon Morgan, had been drinking heavily and began running around barefooted, shouting in such a way that people on both sides thought he "seemed crazy." The noisiest man of the evening, he urged everyone to action. When the mayor hollered at him to tone down, the crazed drunk asked the mayor—a bachelor—whether he wanted his daughter to marry a black. Morgan threatened to kill another man if he did not join the mob.

Then word reached the angry crowd that Bishop had died, about thirty minutes after he had been wounded. That added heat to an already burning hatred, and by the time the mayor came out of the building, the militants had secured a ladder, as well as more arms and more whiskey. Mayor Krum told them of the dangers, the laws being violated, and the possible punishment for breaking those laws, but his comments did not move the men, for in their midst were many of the community's outstanding leaders, including three physicians: Dr. Beal, Dr. James Jennings, and Dr. Thomas Hope. Someone yelled at the mayor, "Get out of the way and go home." Others shouted in agreement. One started swearing at him. Whiskey was also being passed around "profusely," as one newspaper described it.[13]

While the mayor talked, several men raised a ladder against the windowless side of the building, under the direction of Dr. Hope. They planned to reach the wooden roof and set it on fire. As Mayor Krum spoke, rifles began to fire, and some buckshot went through his hat. The ladder did not reach the roof; they tried several other ladders and then tied two ladders together and placed them on the side of the building, reaching the roof. The crowd started chanting, "Burn them out! Burn them out!" The men outside persuaded a youth known only as Okeh to go up the ladder with the flame to light the roof. Okeh delivered drugs for Dr. Hope, and the physician urged Okeh to go up the ladder. Okeh put on several overcoats to partially protect himself from buckshot and bullets. As Okeh started up the ladder, one brave spectator who saw what would happen, went up the ladder after him to put out the flame. A few shots were directed at the would-be fire fighter, and he quickly disappeared. But getting up the ladder to the wooden roof with a burning torch did not turn out to be a simple task, perhaps complicated by the heavy drinking. It took longer than the young man or his followers thought, and as they watched him try to ascend the ladder to set the roof on fire, three or four volunteers from the inside, Lovejoy among them, came into the open and pushed the ladder over, shooting at those at the foot of the ladder.

This happened so quickly that the mob fired only a few wild shots in return. One shot narrowly missed killing the youth, grazing the side of his head. He experienced a sudden and bruising fall to the ground. More shouts came from the crowd and also from some of the spectators anxious for excitement: "Fire the house!" "Burn them out!" "Shoot every Abolitionist in the building if they try to escape!" Another attacker, James Rock, volunteered to take the flame up the ladder. The militants assured him that they would protect him with their weapons. Two of the men covering for him, Dr. Beal and Dr. Jennings, hid with rifles behind a woodpile. The wood, a few barrels and a large, old steam boiler were the only items on the vacant lot next to the building. Rock, outlandishly dressed in top hat and tails, was ready for a big party that night. He already had had several drinks and was carrying a rifle.

In the meantime, Mrs. Frederick Graves, a sickly, small, thin woman, did not know what to do. Her husband, one of Lovejoy's friends, was out of town. Rather than do nothing, she went to the First Presbyterian church, where her husband served as minister, less than half a mile from the warehouse, and started ringing the church bells. During the entire final period of gunfire, the bells of the church continued to toll. Unfortunately, the ringing of the bells brought additions to the mob and more curious spectators who simply wanted to see a show. City Judge William Martin, according to his assertion after the tragedy, went among the spectators trying to get help to stop the violence. He reported: "I found no one who was willing to assist in the suppression of the mob."[14]

At one point in the evening, fifteen-year-old Joseph Brown (later mayor of Alton and St. Louis) slipped into the building with some supplies, particularly bullets. Brown worked part-time for Royal Weller in the Weller shoe store. Earlier that day, Weller told Brown to mold a lot of bullets, in a mold that Weller owned, for possible use in the warehouse that evening. When

Brown entered the warehouse with his bullets, Lovejoy occupied the center of the group, discussing the situation. Some favored surrendering the press rather than shedding more blood, but Lovejoy stood firm and, with a voice shaking with emotion, told them: "We must fight it out, if necessary, to the bitter end. I for one, am willing and ready to lay down my life."

When the second attempt to set the building on fire started, this time by James Rock, those inside knew that they must expose themselves again and attempt to push the ladder over. Lovejoy once more volunteered. Also volunteering were Royal Weller and perhaps Amos Roff. Roff at least followed the other two outside of the building. The difference in this second attempt to start flames on the wooden roof—by putting burning pitch on it—was that the mob leaders knew what to expect from those on the inside. The two armed physicians stationed themselves behind the woodpile, about twenty feet long and four or five feet high, ready to fire. When Lovejoy and Weller came out to push away the ladder once again, rifles cracked. They wounded Weller but not fatally. Five shots hit Lovejoy. He struggled to get inside again and up the flight of stairs. Then he fell down in the counting room and said simply, "My God, I am shot!" His legs hung down the stairs. He died immediately, suffering three shots in the chest, one in the abdomen, and one in the left arm. Someone inside yelled to the mob, perhaps in the hope of sending them home: "They have murdered Elijah Lovejoy!" This caused a tremendous "yell of exultation" from the mob outside, "which shook the very heavens," as Owen Lovejoy wrote about it later.[15]

The roof of the building had been set on fire, and someone advised the defenders to flee quickly, but the mob had not finished its business. Someone suggested that the building should be destroyed. They rolled the old boiler to the side of the building and lit a keg of powder between the boiler and the warehouse, hoping to destroy the structure or at least to blow a big hole in the warehouse. At the same time, two citizens, Edward Keating, a lawyer, and Henry West, a merchant, told Lovejoy's friends that some of the attackers had assured them that if the defenders would leave the building and let the crowd have the press, they would not be harmed. Those inside—demoralized by the death of Lovejoy and with the roof burning over their heads—had no choice.

About the same time, one of the defenders of the press, heavyset William Harned, shouted that Lovejoy had been killed and that the attackers could have the press if those on the inside could leave unmolested. Amos Roff, the stove merchant, went outside to try to get some type of peace agreement, but as soon as he set foot outside the door, they shot him in the ankle. He also suffered a slight wound in his nose, near his eye. Standing at the side of the warehouse, eighteen-year-old J. W. Harned risked gunfire to run into the building to see if his father, William Harned, had been wounded or killed. One man wanted to stay and fight it out to death, but the others quickly outvoted him. As the defenders fled, the mob did not keep its pledge of safe exit and opened fire on the men running for safety. Amazingly, they hit no one. Gilman later recalled: "We were fired on whilst leaving the building, and the outlaws came in and made their gross remarks about the dead lion, whose body then lay in the counting room, and whose blood had consecrated the soil of Alton."[16] One man with the family name of Temple grabbed some wooden type for souvenirs as he hastily exited. A few of those who rushed out locked themselves in a nearby building. On the door someone drew pictures of coffins and wrote: "Ready made coffins for sale."[17] He then listed the names of the people inside.

Two brave men stayed behind. One was Rev. Thaddeus Hurlbut, Lovejoy's associate editor, two years older than Lovejoy. He guarded the body. The other was Weller, the man wounded at the same time they killed Lovejoy. Weller sat on a chair near a stove, washing his bleeding leg. When one of the physicians in the mob, Dr. Hope, volunteered to remove the shot from Weller's leg, the wounded man refused to allow him to do it. Weller said he would rather die. A few minutes later, George Whitney, a local druggist and a Lovejoy ally, spotted Weller. Applying a tourniquet, he saved Weller's life.

Okeh, the first young man to ascend the ladder, some time later had a scar above his eye and claimed he had been hit while ascending the ladder. No one on the scene at the time recalled his being hit there, though a bullet had grazed the side of his head. Some in the crowd volunteered to put out the fire on the roof. Henry West ascended the ladder, carrying water in his silk top hat, to put out the burning tar ball on the roof. Dr. Hope, one of those who claimed to have shot Lovejoy, put water in West's hat. Others broke up the press and threw it into the river. One observer noted that they destroyed the press in an "orderly and quiet sort of way" and that they appeared to be thoroughly enjoying their work. As they methodically destroyed the press, one of the men, Dr. Beal, warned: "Now, boys we've got to stick together. If any one of us is arrested, we must come to the rescue." Later that evening, Dr. Beal threatened to kill every Abolitionist in the city. Dr. Beal, "in pretty good spirits" the whole evening, appeared to be enjoying himself immensely.

After they destroyed the press and threw the parts into the Mississippi River, "the mob poured into the warehouse," in the words of one witness.[18] The curious started to approach Lovejoy's body, guarded by Hurlbut, who told them, "Come in, men. Come in." Alone with the Lovejoy body and the wounded Weller, Hurlbut suddenly jerked away the handkerchief that covered Lovejoy's face, pointed to Lovejoy's body, and shouted, "See your work, brave men!" They fled immediately. It was all over by about two o'clock in the morning.

One sympathetic observer recalled later: "It was a pity that Henry Tanner was not commander that night in place of the aged, mild, and courteous Deacon Enoch Long. The crisis required either vigorous fighting and a Napoleonic movement upon the enemy, or Quaker non-resistance. The half-way policy which was adopted produced its natural unhappy results."[19] Another man inside the warehouse noted: "The thought never entered our minds that the mob was as bad as it turned out to be; and therefore, we did not prepare as we ought to have done."[20]

In a pre-telegraph era, word spread relatively quickly about the Alton disaster. The Peoria newspaper reported: "We learn by the steamboat Ark . . . that as the boat passed Alton on Tuesday night, about 12 o'clock, the church bells were ringing, muskets firing, and a prodigious excitement prevailing. The captain was warned to keep further off, lest random shot might endanger the safety of persons on the boat. He understood that the commotion was produced by the landing of another press for Mr. Lovejoy, and the determination of his friends to protect it, and the equally resolute determination of the mob to destroy it. We shall learn the particulars in a day or two."[21]

Lovejoy's two brothers, Owen and John, alone and armed, stood guard at his home. (Celia Ann and her son were still at another house for safety purposes.) The first disquieting "news" to reach the Lovejoy brothers was Lovejoy's horse returning with no rider. Later that morning, a few brave friends took Lovejoy's body home. Cheers and a few crude shouts greeted those who carried the body through the streets. Dr. Hope, a medical partner of Dr. Beal, shouted at those escorting the body: "I would like to kill every damned Abolitionist fanatic in town!" Owen Lovejoy stood in the doorway when they brought Elijah to his house. Dr. Beal danced a little marching jig ahead of the horse that pulled the Lovejoy body. He pretended to be playing an instrument, and to the delight of spectators, he said, "If I had a fife, I would play a death march for him!"[22]

A day later, on his thirty-fifth birthday, Lovejoy was buried in a field near his home. His brothers reported that he "looked perfectly natural, but a little paler than usual, and a smile still resting upon his lips."[23] For fear of further mob action, Rev. Thomas Lippincott, father-in-law of Gilman, offered only a brief prayer and no further service or ceremony. It was rainy and muddy and cold. There were no flowers, and only a few courageous friends gathered. Stunned by her husband's death, Celia Ann Lovejoy, already seriously ill and now a widow at the age of twenty-four, did not have the strength to witness the simple burial. Lovejoy's grave was dug by "an old Negro gravedigger," William Scott — or William "Scotch" Johnson — who had been born in Scotland.[24] He refused to take any money for digging the grave. In accordance with an old custom, he "collected poke berries and stained with their juice the coffin."[25] Throughout Lovejoy's burial, the bell of the Presbyterian Church gave its solemn, steady message that someone was being interred, the same bell that tolled the night he was murdered.

The ground on the grave had not settled when legal action began.

🐌 8

🐌 Injustice and Aftermath

There is no stranger twist to the entire Lovejoy story than the trials that followed his death, and the fate of the men who killed Lovejoy is another weird climax to this struggle for freedom.

The first man to be tried was Winthrop Gilman, who had defended his property and tried to resist the mob that killed Lovejoy. The charge against him was starting a riot. Gilman told friends that he "thought it was quite singular that he should be indicted for protecting his own life and property."[1] The grand jury specifically charged that Gilman and eleven others "unlawfully, riotously, and routously, and in a violent and tumultuous manner, resisted and opposed an attempt . . . to break up and destroy a printing-press . . . contrary to the form of the statute . . . and against the peace and dignity of the people of the State of Illinois."[2] Gilman asked to be tried separately from the other eleven, and the court granted that request. The others charged were: Enoch Long, Amos Roff, George Walworth, George Whitney, William Harned, John Noble, James Morse, Jr., Henry Tanner, Royal Weller, Reuben Gerry, and Thaddeus Hurlbut.

The legal basis for the grand jury's action, a section of the Illinois Criminal Code, reads: "If two or more persons actually do an unlawful act with force or violence against the person or property of another, with or without a common cause or quarrel, or even do a lawful act, in a violent and tumultuous manner, the

136

persons so offending shall be deemed guilty of a Riot, and on conviction, shall severally be fined not exceeding two hundred dollars, or imprisonment not exceeding six months."[3] There were three attorneys for the government and three for the defendants. The most important prosecuting attorney was Usher Linder, attorney general of the state of Illinois, and he bore partial responsibility for Lovejoy's death because of his encouragement of the lawless elements in Alton.

While Linder as attorney general should have been defending any citizen's right to express whatever views he or she wished, he instead tried to make the issue the fact that Lovejoy's press would be used to fight slavery. For example, Linder questioned Mayor Krum on the witness stand: "Did Mr. Gilman ever tell you what principles that press was intended to advocate?" Linder and the other prosecuting attorneys also called Gilman and the other defenders "fanatics" who should be punished.

Both sides used religious arguments to buttress their cause. The prosecuting attorney for the city of Alton, who worked with Linder, appealed to the jury: "It is lamentable . . . to consider the excesses to which fanaticism, in the name of our holy religion, often drives the best and most intelligent men. If the defendant had been led by the dictates of the religion he adorns . . . how different would have been his conduct. . . . Did he who is God alone — did he, when nailed to the cross, curse his cruel persecutors, and die? Did he oppose violence [with] violence? And yet, gentlemen, the defendant thought [himself] justified by the religion of the Savior."[4]

In summing up the argument to the jury, Linder began by saying that either Gilman and the others were guilty or that the people, including the jurors who tried to destroy the press, were guilty. He clearly appealed to the jurors' desire to have "the other man" guilty. He claimed that the purpose of Lovejoy's press was to promote "fiendish doctrines," and he referred to "this damning doctrine of Abolition." Linder additionally maintained that their going to the mayor for advice showed that Gilman and his friends knew they were wrong: "A man who is conscious that he is acting from right impulses wants no advice; he acts from his own honest convictions."

But Linder's main argument essentially attacked freedom of the press. Of the pro-Lovejoy group, Linder said: "They talk of being friends to good order; lovers of law. Have they not taken the law into their own hands, and violated the laws of man and of God in depriving man of life? And for what? For a press! A printing press! A press brought here to teach the slave rebellion; to excite the slaves to war, to preach murder in the name of religion; to strike dismay in the hearts of people, and spread desolation over the face of this land. Society honors good order more than such a press, sets higher value upon the lives of its citizens than upon a thousand such presses. I might picture for you the Negro, his passions excited by the doctrines intended to have been furthered by that press. You might just as well place yourselves in the fangs of a wild beast. I might portray to you the scenes which would exist in our neighbor states from the influence of that press: The father aroused to see the last gasp of his dying child, as it lies in its cradle, weltering in its own blood; and the husband, awakened from his last sleep by the shrieks of his wife, as she is brained to the earth. I might paint to you a picture which would cause the devil to start back with fright—and still fall short of the awful reality which would be caused by the doctrines which this press was intended to promote."

A friend of Lovejoy observed that Linder and the prosecution "resorted to all the low intrigues and petty cavilings their prejudices and vulgar minds could invent. They had an opportunity of delivering themselves of all the bitter animosity and acrimonious feelings which they entertained against the abolitionists."[5] But the Linder oratory could not overcome the facts, even in Alton. The jury deliberated only fifteen minutes and found Gilman not guilty. The state then dropped its charges against the others.

In another strange twist of justice, the leaders of the mob were also slated for trial. Immediately after the slaying, some assumed that the assailants would flee Alton. A Quincy, Illinois, leader urged the governor of Illinois to "offer an award of some $5,000 or $10,000 to apprehend the leaders of the mob."[6] But with one exception, they all stayed in Alton, obviously sensing no need to hide. Attorney General Linder served as the primary defense attorney for those who had killed Lovejoy and entered the Gilman warehouse. Alexander Botkin, one of the leaders of the anti-Lovejoy forces, served as foreman of this jury. The facts brought out were essentially the same; they fought over the same issues once again; and the result came out the same: not guilty. Despite the crimes committed in plain view, not one person paid a penny fine, and not one person went to prison for a single day.

Attorney General Linder's bright political future soon ended. His heavy drinking and bad reputation, due in large part to the Lovejoy tragedy, led him downhill. In later years, he served in the Illinois House of Representatives again and remained politically active, but he experienced a dim ending to what once had been considered a brilliant political future. He maintained his hostility toward African Americans throughout his life. More than ten years after the close of the Civil War, he wrote that our government "was a white man's government, made by white men for the benefit of the white race." He always maintained that he was "severely assailed and maligned" unjustly for the part he and John Hogan had played in the whole Lovejoy episode. The two of them, he said, had done "all that mortal man could do to bring about peace between these hostile elements."[7]

Four men later claimed the "honor" of having fired the shot that killed Lovejoy. One was James Rock, who had gone up the ladder armed. Dr. Beal and Dr. Jennings, who had taken a position behind the woodpile with rifles pointing at the door from which Lovejoy came, each claimed to have hit Lovejoy. The fourth to claim the "honor" was Virginia-born Dr. Hope, whose position during the action is not known, other than that he participated actively with the mob. Since Lovejoy suffered five wounds, it is possible that all had a part in it. When all the factors are weighed, it seems likely that the two doctors hidden behind the woodpile were responsible for Lovejoy's murder. However, for three of the four of these men, the future would not be happy.

The panic of 1837 had already hit Alton when the news of the Lovejoy slaying spread everywhere. Alton became known as a town of lawlessness. River traffic went to St. Louis and other towns. Instead of passing St. Louis in growth, as seemed likely, Alton started losing ground. Gilman, who later became a successful businessman in New York City, left Alton. Real estate values plunged. One twenty-five-thousand-dollar piece of property soon sold for two thousand dollars. Overnight, Alton changed from being almost the largest city in the Midwest to a town losing its population and its economic base. Typical of the editorial reaction to the Lovejoy slaying was the *Lynn* (Mass.) *Record*: "Who but a savage or cold-hearted murderer would now go to Alton? Meanness, infamy, and guilt are attached to the very name. Hereafter, when a criminal is considered too bad for any known punishment, it will be said of him: 'He ought to be banished to Alton.' "[8] People in the community began blaming the mob leaders more and more for the city's decline, and most of these agitators found it convenient to leave Alton.

Dr. Jennings left town almost immediately, even before the trials. His motivation for leaving we can only guess. He died in a knife fight in a barroom in Vicksburg, Mississippi, several years later, according to a published report not easy to confirm.

Dr. Beal, the roughest talking of the three physicians involved, eventually went southwest to join the Texas Rangers. Whether he actually joined them is not clear. He is said to have been captured by the Comanche Indians and, one report asserts, burned to death. Another published story said that the account of his capture by the Indians was only a cover-up, that he had actually been killed by his own men. Both versions were published in Illinois and Missouri. The *Magazine of Western History* reported that in 1845–46, he served as "acting surgeon" to a regiment of the Texas Rangers and that one of his own men killed him.[9] Texas, however, has no record of his service, unless a private with the doctor's name is the same person. It is possible he did medical work for the Rangers but did not join.

Rock went from prison to prison—at one point he served time in the Ohio State Penitentiary—and finally cut his own throat in the Missouri Penitentiary, jailed there for attempted burglary and the attempted murder of a woman.

Dr. Hope, the only one of the four to weather the storm, became mayor of Alton. In later years, he ran for Congress. What Dr. Hope became most known for, however, occurred five years after Lovejoy's death, when he served as a second for James Shields in a duel Shields scheduled with Abraham Lincoln. The duel, set to take place on an island not far from Alton, was called off at the last minute. Shields had a largely undistinguished political career, but his military service in the war with Mexico made him enough of a hero that he became the only American ever to serve as a U.S. Senator from three states. His near-duel with Lincoln occurred as a result of letters published in a Springfield, Illinois, newspaper that Shields believed questioned his honor. Shields mistakenly believed Lincoln had written the letters.

When in 1858, Lincoln and Stephen A. Douglas had their famous debate in Alton, Dr. Hope, believing both were too sympathetic to the antislavery cause, opposed both of them.

When Douglas got up to speak, Dr. Hope shouted a question about slavery in the territories. Douglas replied: "You will get an answer in the course of my remarks."[10] The crowd cheered Douglas and booed Dr. Hope, an indication that his popularity in Alton had dimmed. During the Civil War, Dr. Hope experienced being "detained for some time" in prison for his outspoken views in opposition to the Union cause.[11]

William Carr, one of those indicted with the group that attacked the warehouse, approached an Alton citizen, James Morse, Jr., "and asked him if he had given his [Carr's] name to the grand jury—or whether he had testified against him. He replied in the negative, whereupon Carr called him a damned liar, and as Morse turned to go into the store, struck him with a club that nearly brought him to the ground."[12] Morse said that he planned to ask for prosecution of Carr, but there is no record of such a prosecution.

Royal Weller, the shoe store operator who ran out with Lovejoy the second time they tried to stop the roof burning, had a limp the rest of his life from the leg wound he suffered. He visited Lovejoy's widow after she had moved to Cincinnati and after Weller had moved to Detroit. In December 1841, four years after Lovejoy's death, the clerk of Wayne County, Michigan, apparently issued a marriage certificate to Weller, forty-three years old, and Celia Ann Lovejoy, twenty-eight years old.[13] It developed into a troubled marriage, and Royal Weller and Celia Ann Lovejoy eventually separated, though there is no record of a divorce. She resumed use of the name Lovejoy, and in a lengthy autobiographical letter many years later, Celia Ann and Elijah's son Edward do not mention the marriage.

A few years after the marriage of Weller and Celia Ann, a strange episode developed in which Weller, as administrator of the estate of Elijah Lovejoy, sued Owen Lovejoy for the items Owen took after Elijah's death and Celia's hasty departure to her parents' home in St. Charles, Missouri. According to the testimony of two people, Celia Ann told Owen to take the things, but Weller sued him for "one full suit of Ten dollar Lion's cloth clothes; one Lion's hair over-coat, one cow, one cooking stove, and one table . . . one volume of Lord Byron's works, one volume of Hazlitt's Extracts of the British Poets, eight volumes of Rollen's Ancient History, Pollack's Course of time; Gems of Literature . . . three large garden hoes, two razors, one Strap and Shaving Apparatus, one ivory holder, one Sand box . . . one Sitle umbrella, one Spade . . . the same being of great value have been embezzled by the said Owen Lovejoy."[14]

Owen had lived with Elijah and Celia Ann and had worked for his brother at the newspaper with no known agreement on wages, more concerned with the cause of freedom and life and death issues than with compensation. The Weller-Owen Lovejoy legal battle escalated after Weller's opening shot and Owen's subsequent legal resistance. Weller sued Owen for a year's board, for washing and ironing, and even for the use of fire and candles. Owen Lovejoy countered that he had paid out "divers sums of money and was put to great trouble and expense . . . and paid debts against the estate out of his own funds" with the expectation that he would be repaid. In the same document, Owen charged that "Weller is a wasteful and prodigal person unfit to have the management of said estate."[15] Weller's efforts got him nothing other than legal bills, and probably embarrassed Celia Ann. Weller later was committed to the Central Hospital for the Insane in Jacksonville, Illinois, and died there in 1859.

Celia Ann remained in a state of shock for several days after the death of her husband, but as soon as she could, she moved to her parents' home in St. Charles. On April 16, 1838, Owen Lovejoy visited her and wrote that she had a healthy baby girl born March 5, four months after Elijah's death. Celia Ann's mother came from a slaveholding family that maintained strong feelings against the Abolitionists, and she had never been pleased with her daughter's marriage to Lovejoy. Four years after Lovejoy's death, Celia Ann, who had been seriously ill for about ten weeks, wrote: "Mother did not come near me, only three or four times. She said it was all the doings of the Abolitionists. She expected they would kill me."[16] Other family difficulties can be judged by the simple statement, "Now insane in Illinois," on the church records of the First Presbyterian Church of St. Charles with regard to Celia Ann's sister.

Celia Ann went with her children to Maine to be with her husband's relatives and eventually moved to Cincinnati where the *Observer* had been published after its Alton demise. A careful researcher of the Lovejoy family reports that the "daughter died as an infant" but does not give the source for that information.[17] A year after the birth, she seemed in good health in Maine, while the son, Edward, had a "violent fit," and Celia Ann was described as "pretty quiet."[18] In August 1839, Celia Ann was traveling with Edward and not with a daughter.

In Cincinnati, Celia Ann tried running a boardinghouse that did not become a financial success. The Ohio Antislavery Society passed a resolution to make a national appeal for funds. The printed appeal noted that Celia Ann is "now in destitute circumstances and very poor health on account of her sufferings."[19] In 1840, Celia Ann's mother, who still hated the Abolitionist cause, joined Celia Ann in Cincinnati. Celia Ann wrote: "I felt it my duty to do all in my power to make her happy. When my house began to fill up with boarders, they were of course abolitionists. This she considered a disgrace. . . . She persecuted me all she could, which was not a little. She required me to renounce my Antislavery principles or she should not live with me. I always told her I could not . . . do such a wicked thing. . . . I did not receive anything but reproach from her and threats. . . . I tryed to reason the case with her but it did no good. My sickness [involved] termination of blood to the brain. I was in fits and spasms. I did not expect to live. . . . For ten weeks I was only lifted from the bed to the chair with the utmost care. . . . During this time mother did not come near me. Mr. Weller remained with me and nursed me faithfully and suffered everything on my account. Mother's hostility toward him was dreadful." Celia Ann then talks about "the girls" — probably a reference to the two female slaves owned by Mrs. French — and her mother taking them without Celia Ann's consent to St. Charles. "Mother now stands committed as a kidnapper. . . . By the laws of Ohio it is a penitentiary offence. . . . I will leave you to imagine what my feelings and struggles have been during all this and in my low state of health." She added: "Brother Weller is quite well. He was out to see me the other day."[20] She wrote this eight months before the marriage license was issued in Michigan.

Later Celia Ann traveled to Canada and the Pacific Coast but maintained little contact with the movement against slavery. On at least one occasion, she returned to the Midwest. She died July 10, 1870, at the age of fifty-seven. Before she died, she visited one of Lovejoy's friends. He reported that she "passed several days at my house, a broken-down, prematurely old person, possessed of hardly a trace of her early beauty."[21]

Lovejoy's son, Edward, two years old when his father died, lived as an adult in California and Nevada. He experienced early financial difficulty, but in later life, his economic circumstances improved. On March 4, 1890, Edward wrote on a letterhead titled "E. P. Lovejoy, General Merchandise and Produce, Wabuska, Nevada." Writing to the husband of his father's sister, he said that he would be fifty-four years old in a few days and that in his life he had "hardly [had] an ungratified desire." He added: "Aside from the companionship of my Sainted Mother, I have never had the slightest personal acquaintance with any blood relative since childhood. My lot has been cast entirely among strangers. So I have lived and so I expect to die. That this was so I have regretted for my Mother's sake. Singlehanded she battled with poverty . . . [to] educate her boy and whatever there may be of good in him he owes to her teaching and example. . . . She lived to see her boy emerge from poverty and obscurity and serve her in her declining years with everything she desired."[22]

Edward described his mother as "a very nervous woman which was hardly to be wondered at considering the trials and tribulations she had gone through." He tells of going with his mother from Cincinnati to Oberlin in Ohio, to Chicago for two years, and on to New York State: Fowlerville, Rochester, and Buffalo. Then they traveled to Chesterfield in Greene County, Illinois, to Iowa, to a place near Quincy, and to Upper Alton in the fall of 1849. Edward attended Shurtleff College there (founded by an opponent of his father) until the fall of 1851. They moved to Keokuk, Iowa, where Celia Ann bought a farm and took in boarders. They stayed there for two years before moving to California. He mentions that his mother "was troubled greatly with bronchitis and hysteria,"[23] but her health improved when she went to California.

Edward became a lawyer and was elected as a justice of the peace, then elected and reelected as a district attorney and a county judge. He bought the only newspaper in the county and ran it for nine years. Like his father, he tried his hand at poetry. Edward failed in two business enterprises after earlier successes, ending up working temporarily "as a common laborer" for the railroad. Then he became the postmaster at Wabuska, Nevada, and entered into business successfully. He noted: "I am in possession of considerable property, own about 1500 acres of land, some cattle and horses, but I owe a great deal of money, about half the value of the property. The problem now is to pay off the indebtedness. . . . I was married on October 30, 1869 to a lady 11 years younger than myself. We have no children. My wife was confined in 1871 and although a healthy, strong woman the Physicians were compelled to take the child away with instruments and I believe killed him in the womb. They said it was impossible for her to deliver it. I was heartbroken. It was such a large, strong infant and the picture of me."[24]

While Edward barely got to know his father, during his years of newspaper work, he showed some of his father's same spirit and attitude. Of a political candidate, he commented: "A. J. Doolittle is an independent candidate for the Assembly in Nevada. He is rightly named. He did little when at Douglas City, and we imagine he will do little in the election."[25] But more significantly, when a legislator attacked Japanese Americans, Lovejoy rose to their defense and noted: "The past teaches us that mere appeals to prejudice yield no lasting victories."[26] And when a school district refused to integrate African Americans, he attacked this "denial of civil rights to negroes."[27] His father would have applauded these editorial thrusts. Edward died in 1891 at the age of fifty-five. A Lovejoy researcher, Rev. Robert Tabscott, appropriately a Presbyterian minister, found Edward's gravestone in Dayton, Nevada.

Edward Beecher, Lovejoy's friend and supporter who headed Illinois College in Jacksonville, heard the news of Lovejoy's death in Jacksonville and wrote to Lovejoy's brother: "From Alton will his voice go out till it has reached the utmost bounds of the civilized world. His enemies have failed in their purpose and he has triumphed in his fall."[28] Beecher went on to become a powerful voice against slavery as a nationally prominent preacher. Nine years after the end of the Civil War, Edward Beecher was asked to appear at a meeting honoring Lovejoy several hundred miles from his home. He responded: "It will give me great pleasure to prepare a memorial of the Martyr Lovejoy," but as to attending the convention, "I have no salary and support my family by writing. . . . I am obliged to avoid all needless expenses."²⁹ Beecher's sister, Harriet Beecher Stowe, absorbed from her brother the facts and the passion from the Lovejoy slaying. She "found time to follow carefully [the] . . . battle around the freedom of the press that was fought in Illinois that involved her brother Edward and his close friend Elijah P. Lovejoy."³⁰ Twenty-nine years old when the mob killed Lovejoy, fourteen years later she wrote the book *Uncle Tom's Cabin* that stirred the nation further against slavery.

One of the presses that the mob threw into the river remained intact in the river for twenty-one years when someone pulled it out and refurbished it, selling it to a man named W. R. Mead for thirty-five dollars. Mead resold it to the publisher of the *Cresco Plain Dealer* in Howard County, Iowa.³¹ Eventually, the press came back to Alton, as a display item at the *Alton Telegraph*.

Lovejoy had two brothers and a sister living with him in Alton at the time of his slaying. When his mother heard of his death, she wrote immediately to the other three, asking: "Are you yet alive?" She added: "Don't, my dear children, harbor any revengeful feelings toward the murderers of your dear brother."³² A month after Elijah's death, Joseph Lovejoy wrote from Maine to his brother Owen, still in Alton: "Mother is very much sustained under this awful calamity. Sybil [a sister] is now much better but has been quite sick since the news of the death of Brother P[arish]." He added: "I shall want to visit Alton and assist in bringing these perpetrators to justice if possible."³³ Joseph went on to become the editor of three antislavery journals published in Maine, none of which had wide circulation.

Owen Lovejoy, nine years younger than Elijah, swore over the body of his dead bother to devote his life to the cause of freeing the slaves. His immediate plans were to become a member of the Episcopalian clergy, but when the bishop asked him to sign a pledge not to discuss Abolitionism, he refused. The Presbyterians indicated a willingness to accept him, but he eventually became a Congregational minister and a powerful foe of slavery. One month after the tragedy, Owen Lovejoy wrote to a friend: "My brother has done more dying than he could living, and horrid as was the sacrifice, all things considered I cannot regret that it was made. In a conversation we had a short time before his death, I advised him to stand firm at his post; although I did not then think that this tragic result would follow, I still think he did his duty in remaining in Alton. If called upon, I trust God I shall be willing to follow the same course."[34] In later years, he actively supported the Underground Railroad, served in Congress, and became a strong supporter of Lincoln.

During the period immediately prior to the Civil War, slavery became such a controversial issue that even on the floor of the U.S. House and Senate, discussion of the issue rarely occurred because the rules prohibited it. Reasonable alternatives to war became less likely because they could not be discussed. A member of the U.S. House who continued discussion of the issue—despite the rules—was Representative Owen Lovejoy of Illinois. On April 5, 1860, one year and ten days before the Civil War began, he rose in the House of Representatives, and the official record shows the following discourse took place:

> *Mr. Lovejoy*: The House has been occupied for several days in the discussion of the subject of polygamy. The Republican party, of which I am a member, stands pledged since 1856 to the extermination, so far as the Federal Government has the power, of the twin relics of barbarism, slavery and polyga-
> my. . . . Now, sir, as we anticipate a death blow having been given to one of these twins, I propose to pay my respects to the other. I want to see them both strangled and go down together, as they both richly deserve.
> *Mr. Cobb* [of Alabama]: I rise to a question of order.
> *The Chairman*: The gentleman will state his question of order.
> *Mr. Cobb*: I was going to raise a question of order upon the right of the gentleman to discuss [slavery] . . . under the new rule

we have adopted. However, I will not interfere; the gentleman
may go on with his speech. . . .

Mr. Lovejoy: Slaveholding has been justly designated as the sum
of all villainy. Put every crime perpetrated among men into a
moral crucible, and dissolve and combine them all, and the re-
sultant amalgam is slaveholding. It has the violence of robbery.

A Member: You are joking.

Mr. Lovejoy: No, sir; I am speaking in dead earnest, before God,
God's own truth. . . . I hold that the extreme men, as they are
called, on this question, are the only men who have the logic
of it. I am right, or the fire-eaters are right. If slavery is right
in Virginia, it is right in Kansas. If it is wrong in Kansas, it is
wrong everywhere. . . . The principle of enslaving human beings because they are inferior is this: If a man is a cripple, trip
him up; if he is old and weak, and bowed with the weight of
years, strike him for he cannot strike back; if idiotic, take advantage of him. This, sir, is the doctrine of Democrats, and
the doctrine of devils as well; and there is no place in the uni-
verse, outside the five points of hell and the Democratic party,
where the practice and prevalence of such doctrines would not
be a disgrace. . . . (Laughter)

(Mr. Lovejoy had advanced into the area, and occupied the space
fronting the Democratic benches.)

Mr. Pryor [of Virginia] (advancing from the Democratic side of
the House toward the area where Mr. Lovejoy stood): The gentleman from Illinois [Mr. Lovejoy] shall not approach this side
of the House, shaking his fists, and talking in the way he has
talked. It is bad enough to be compelled to sit here and hear
him utter his treasonable and insulting language. But he shall
not, sir, come upon this side of this House. . . .

Mr. Potter [of Wisconsin]: We listened to gentlemen upon the
other side for eight weeks, when they denounced the members
upon this side with violent and offensive language. We listened to
them quietly, and heard them through. And now, sir, this side
shall be heard, let the consequences be what they may. . . .

(Thirty or forty of the members from both sides of the House
gathered in the area about Mr. Lovejoy and Mr. Pryor, and
there was increased confusion). . . .

The Chairman [Mr. Washburne of Maine]: The Chair calls the Committee [of the Whole House] to order; and if gentlemen do not come to order, he will call the Speaker to the chair, and report the disorder to the House. . . . The Speaker will take the chair. . . .

The Speaker: The Chair requests gentlemen to respect the authority of the House, and take their seats.

Mr. Barksdale [of Mississippi]: Order that black-hearted scoundrel and nigger-stealing thief to take his seat, and this side of the House will do it.

(Cries of "Sit down!" "Sit down!" from all sides of the House) . . .

(Members gradually withdrew from the open area in front of the Speaker's chair, and resumed their seats. Order being at length restored.)

(Lovejoy then resumed his remarks.)

Mr. Gartrell [of Georgia] (in his seat): This man is crazy. . . .

Mr. Barksdale [to Lovejoy]: You stand there today an infamous, perjured villain. [They accused Owen Lovejoy of perjury because he swore to uphold the Constitution and they said the Constitution protected slavery.]

(Calls to order)

Mr. Ashmore [of South Carolina]: Yes, he is a perjured villain; and he perjures himself every hour he occupies a seat on this floor.

(Renewed calls to order). . . .

Mr. Lovejoy: You may kill Cassius M. Clay, as you threaten to do. . . . You may shed his blood, as you shed the blood of my brother on the banks of the Mississippi twenty years ago—and what then? I am here today, thank God, to vindicate the principles baptized in his blood. . . . I am going to invoke the aid of the General Government to protect me, as an American citizen, in my rights as an American citizen. I can go to England today, and in London . . . discuss the question of a monarchical government as compared with a republican form of government. . . . But I cannot go into a slave State and open my lips in regard to the question of slavery—

Mr. Martin [of Virginia]: No; we would hang you higher than Haman. . . .

Mr. Barksdale: The meanest slave in the South is your superior. (Cries of "Order!" from the Republican side). . . .

Mr. Lovejoy: Now gentlemen, I know you are in a good mood to take a little advice. (Laughter) I tell you, I love you all. (Renewed laughter)

Mr. McQueen [of Southern Carolina]: I utterly repudiate your love. . . .

Mr. Lovejoy: We shall not push you. If you say that you want a quarter of a century, you can have it; if you want half a century, you can have it. But I insist that this system ultimately must be extinguished. . . . I am willing to concede that you are as brave as other men, although I do not think you show it by this abusive language, because brave men are always calm and self-possessed. . . .

Mr. Martin [of Virginia]: And if you come among us, we will do with you as we did with John Brown—hang you as high as Haman. I say that as a Virginian.

Mr. Lovejoy: I have no doubt of it.

In his successful race for the U.S. House, Owen Lovejoy was endorsed by the *Western Citizen*. The newspaper said that it was fitting that the brother of Elijah Lovejoy should serve in Congress, and "then let it be said that Illinois has repented."[35] One published, but unconfirmed, report says that when Lincoln signed the Emancipation Proclamation in 1863, freeing the slaves, he asked that Owen Lovejoy, Elijah's brother, be present. When Owen Lovejoy died in 1864, Lincoln immediately responded: "Lovejoy was the best friend I had in Congress."[36] In a tribute to Owen Lovejoy in the House of Representatives, the powerful Congressman Thaddeus Stevens said: "It must be remembered that early in life he saw a beloved brother murdered by the northern minions" of slavery.[37] Private funeral services were held at Lovejoy's farm near Princeton, Illinois, officiated appropriately by the Rev. Edward Beecher.

President Lincoln appointed the other Lovejoy brother present at the slaying as U.S. consul in Peru. In a letter to Lincoln written from Peru twenty-seven years after the tragedy, John Lovejoy spoke of "the memory of my brother."[38] Forty-nine years after the slaying, John Lovejoy—then near eighty years of age—wrote to his sister Elizabeth: "The Republican party did a noble work under Lincoln, but since his time they have been getting worse and worse and now worship the golden calves."[39] The sister with Lovejoy the night of his death became Mrs. H. L. Hammond of Evanston, Illinois. Fifty-four years after her brother's murder when she was seventy-six years old, she wrote about that night: "It was a shock that was before me for years."[40]

It was a shock for the nation also. No one event up to that time had mobilized antislavery sentiment like the death of Lovejoy. The trials in Alton found no one guilty, but public opinion around the nation did not share that verdict.

🕭 9

🕭 The Nation Is Stirred

Elijah Lovejoy's death rocked the nation in opposition to slavery and in behalf of free speech.

Lovejoy became the first U.S. martyr to freedom of the press, and as President Herbert Hoover stated one hundred years later: "Elijah Parish Lovejoy was killed while defending free speech and free press in the United States. Since his martyrdom no man has openly challenged free speech and free press in America."[1] That Hoover observation fails to note many subsequent free speech battles, but his praise of the cause of free speech Elijah Lovejoy would have applauded.

Those who killed Lovejoy and destroyed his printing press thought they were helping the cause of slavery, but they could not have helped the antislavery cause more. His death became one of the two greatest boosts the antislavery movement had from the day of independence to the outbreak of the Civil War, the other being the publication of *Uncle Tom's Cabin*. Writing in 1981, historian Milton Rugoff observed: "The shots fired in Alton on November 7, 1837, would be . . . the beginning of the Civil War."[2] If Lovejoy had lived and published his newspaper unmolested, he would have influenced his small readership, but nothing he could have done alive could have furthered the cause as much as his death.

Newspapers all over the United States condemned the Lovejoy murder; mass meetings were held, sermons preached, lectures given. Several newspapers printed offers of people to go to Alton and continue the newspaper. One wrote: "Being a practical printer, I offer myself to go and print that paper for Mrs. Lovejoy." He said that people should volunteer "though one editor after another should be shot down."[3] Seven weeks later, on December 26, 1837, the next issue of the Alton *Observer* did come out—printed in Cincinnati. It commented simply: " 'Might is right' is our modern code, and murder has become a pastime." The newspaper, edited and published by antislavery forces, appeared for four months and then quietly died. Lovejoy's death also evoked poems and hymns of tribute, many published, many more unpublished. A poem sent to an Indiana publication described his death as "a thunderbolt to tyrants,"[4] and almost all the poems spoke of the disgrace to Alton. A poem in the *Liberator* was titled simply "The City of Blood."[5]

The two major antislavery publications of the nation, the *Liberator* and the *Emancipator*, were stunned by the death of Lovejoy. They printed black column markers similar to those that newspapers used after the assassination of Abraham Lincoln. In a day when most articles in newspapers had no headings, and those headings that did appear were simply in the capital letters of the type size used in the article below, the *Liberator*'s headlines screamed: "Horrid Tragedy! Blood Crieth!" For weeks afterwards, the death of Lovejoy and the national reaction to it dominated the journals. In fact, an avalanche of editorials greeted the nation as word spread about Lovejoy's slaying. The *Emancipator* put out an "extra" and noted that their editors had seen journalistic tributes to Lovejoy in more than two hundred newspapers, and they added: "We do not suppose we have even seen one-half of the testimonies that have been published."[6] The *Emancipator* reprinted all or part of the editorials from 161 newspapers from both the South and the North.

Here are a few typical editorial comments from around the nation:

Philadelphia Observer: Lovejoy's death "has called forth from every part of the land a burst of indignation which has not had its parallel in this country since the battle of Lexington, 1775. . . . The most decided expressions of disapprobation . . . are from the slaveholding states. With a large list of southern papers before us, we find not one attempt at an apology for the murderous outrage."[7]

New York American: "If this American bloodshed in the defense of freedom of the press and the right of every American citizen to think, speak and print his own honest opinions—be not signally vindicated, our representative institutions, our boasted freedom . . . will become, and deserves to become, the scoff and derision of the world."[8]

Pittsburgh Times: "The Alton murder has made ten thousand accessions to the cause of Abolition."[9]

Painesville (Ohio) *Republican*: "We can hardly find language severe enough to express our utter abhorrence of such dastardly, wicked conduct."[10]

National Gazette (Washington, D.C.): "We shall become the pitiable and despised laughing stock of the world if such desperate acts of bloody tyranny find the support of Americans."[11]

Boston Cabinet: "The spirit of slave-holding is the spirit of murder."[12]

New Yorker: "What right have five hundred or five thousand to interfere with the lawful expression of a free man's sentiments. . . . He had as perfect and absolute a right to proclaim and defend his sentiments in Illinois, where nine-tenths may be opposed to them, as though all were enthusiastic in their favour; and he who would deny . . . this right is an enemy to freedom."[13]

Newark Daily Advertiser: "The innocent blood shed at Alton, unavenged, must remain an indelible national stain."[14]

New York Journal of Commerce: "The enemies of Abolition must be very stupid indeed if they expect to put down [Abolition] in this free country by mob violence."[15]

Boston Daily Advocate: "Let his memory be embalmed. The blood of that innocent man will not sink into the ground."[16]

Boston Atlas: "Alton has far outrun Vicksburgh [*sic*] for a reputation for blood and infamy."[17]

Columbus (Ohio) *Journal and Register*: "Alton's only course to free their city from the lasting stigma is to convict the mob leaders."[18]

Massachusetts Spy: "Let her name [Alton] be a by-word and a reproach throughout the nation. Her hands are reeking with innocent blood."[19]

Cincinnati Journal: "Alton! Alton! . . . Mobs have now made thee a by-word in the land. . . . Thou art a polluted thing—blood is on thy garments. Liberty has found a grave in thy bosom. But hush—speak not—a mob is on the throne."[20]

Typical of many southern newspapers, the *Cumberland Presbyterian*, published in Tennessee, differentiated between Lovejoy's views and his rights: "Widely as our sentiments on the subject of abolition differ from those of Mr. Lovejoy . . . we cannot but mourn in bitterness of soul over this horrible catastrophe. . . . The gag laws of Europe are mildness itself, compared to the bloody tragedy at Alton."[21] Also in a slave state, the *Louisville Journal* said: "Violence, outrage and persecution will inflame their [the Abolitionists'] zeal, enlarge their numbers, and increase the power of their dangerous doctrines."[22]

Many other newspapers echoed similar sentiments. There were a few newspapers critical of Lovejoy, but the overwhelming sentiment, in the North and in the South, condemned the mob:

Louisville Herald: "The Mississippi, for a century to come, though it may pour a constant flood, will not pour enough to wash out the disgrace of the horrid murder of Alton."[23]

St. Louis Commercial Bulletin: "His martyrdom will be celebrated by every Abolitionist in the land, and the only consolation we have is that it was inflicted upon him in a non-slaveholding State."[24]

Caledonian (Vermont): "Let the emigrant avoid . . . this Sodom of the West [Alton], lest if he should tarry in it, the wrath of insulted heaven in fire and water should descend and destroy the place with its wicked, pusillanimous and shameless inhabitants."[25]

Baltimore Chronicle: Lovejoy is "a martyr of the very highest public importance."[26]

Jeffersonville (Iowa) *Courier*: "This outrage will fly like the wind to every part of the world. We hope that every individual engaged in the late mob at Alton may be made to suffer."[27]

New York Observer: "Personal liberty is gone, if every man must, on pain of death, do just what the multitude happens to think prudent." (The *Observer* also criticized Lovejoy for taking up arms.)[28]

New York Baptist Register: "Woe to the State of Illinois. We believe the frown of Heaven will rest upon her, and her infamy will be inscribed as with flaming capitals in the skies."[29]

The *Missouri Republican* offered a different perspective: "Everyone must regret this unfortunate occurrence but the guilt . . . will ever rest with those who madly and obstinately persisted in the attempt to establish an abolitionist press."[30] One of the few newspapers critical of Lovejoy, the *Republican*, which had urged the citizens of Alton to get rid of Lovejoy, said: "At each time no violence was shown except to demand the press." The *Pittsburgh Gazette* quoted the St. Louis newspaper and heatedly condemned its statement about there being no violence if Lovejoy would just have given up the press: "We can tell that editor that thousands of men have been hung for highway robbery who most conscientiously could say: 'At each time no violence was shown, except to demand the traveller's money.'"

The *Missouri Argus*, also published in St. Louis, called the death "lamentable" but observed: "The infatuated editor of the Alton Observer has at length fallen victim to his obstinacy in the cause of the Abolitionists. Disregarding the known and expressed sentiments of a large portion of the citizens of Alton, in relation to his incendiary publication, and, as it would seem, bent upon his own destruction."[31] The *New York Evening Post* responded: "We cannot forbear expressing in the strongest language our condemnation of the manner in which the *Missouri Argus* speaks of this bloody event. The right to discuss freely and openly . . . is a right so clear and certain . . . that without it we must fall at once into despotism or anarchy."[32] The *Argus* published only two paragraphs in the next issue after the tragedy a few miles away, and in later editions, not a word. In the capital city of Missouri, the *Jeffersonian* published nothing about Lovejoy's death. The man who had stirred such emotions in Missouri merited not a sentence.

Another place where few expressed public comment was Lovejoy's own state, Illinois. Opinion remained so divided on the slavery issue that only three editors ventured to comment. The *Illinois Temperance Herald*, which Lovejoy supported so avidly, printed not a word about his death. The *Illinois State Register* of Vandalia, the state's capital city, said, "We forbear comment," though they feebly added that "in the supremacy of the laws alone is security."[33] The *Alton Telegraph*, printed during the early evening hours of the night the mob killed Lovejoy, came out the next morning expressing hope that the "great public meeting" arranged by Linder and Hogan would cause the "removal of the excitement" in the community.[34] The following week's edition published the mayor's limited factual account of what happened and nothing more. An incident that stunned the nation and caused mass protests went largely ignored in the *Alton Telegraph*. The *Boston Daily Advocate* noted the *Telegraph*'s motto: "Men should with frankness stand by their principles, and not be frightened by the number of opponents." The *Advocate* commented: "Lovejoy dared to act upon it; the *Telegraph* only keeps it as a motto."[35] Two weeks later, the *Telegraph* published an editorial about the silk problem and about railroads. The week after that, the *Telegraph* responded to criticism that it did not publish national reactions to what had happened in Alton: "Their republication here would probably revive the now subsiding excitement. . . . We are persuaded that our true course is to let the subject rest for the present."[36] A few weeks later, the

Telegraph noted a new Illinois publication, the *Backwoodsman* (Shawneetown), which said it would be open to all opinions except it would not tolerate "discussion of the question of slavery or abolition, in any shape whatsoever."[37] Ultimately, a nation that could not talk about its big problem fought over it. Illinois was not the South, but it was close. (Even in later years, when Lincoln signed the Emancipation Proclamation, the Illinois Legislature passed a resolution condemning his action.)

Two notable Illinois exceptions to this silence on Lovejoy's death were the *Peoria Register* and the *Northwestern Gazette and Galena Advertiser*. The *Peoria Register*'s comments are particularly interesting because it stoutly defended slavery. "It is folly," the newspaper noted, "to connect Abolition with this tragedy. All our readers know that we have expressed ourselves as decidedly against the doctrines of the Abolitionists as any press in the state. We are this moment a slaveowner, possessing that species of property in another state, and we mean to keep it. But a man may write and publish against slavery until his mind and fortune are exhausted, without any hindrance from us."[38] The Peoria newspaper's story said that Alton had been "surrendered by her police into the hands of the mob. Brute force is stronger than the law, and the fate of the city is sealed." The *Peoria Register* charged the mob with becoming "the assassins of the character of the city. Was it for this our fathers endangered their lives? The murdered Lovejoy had done these ruffians no injury." The newspaper praised those who stood with Lovejoy in defending the press: "Alton is unworthy of such men. They should shake the dust from off their feet, and retire to a spot where their valor would be cherished. . . . The thanks of a nation are due them. Their patriotism will live throughout all time, while the names and memory of the chief actors in the mob will stink in the nostrils of men everywhere."[39]

The *Northwestern Gazette and Galena Advertiser* expressed

shock that Lovejoy had been shot "at the hands of a lawless mob! We want language to express our utter abhorrence and condemnation of these whole proceedings. . . . This, too, in a town which boasts of its morality and good order. Their boasts hereafter may be considered as those of the Pharisee. The city should be pointed at as a 'whited sepulchre . . . filled with dead men's bones.' We boast that ours is a land of liberty and yet slavery is the only thing which must not be condemned!" The Galena newspaper also criticized the other newspapers of the state for not condemning the mob violence. It particularly aimed its verbal shots at the newspapers in St. Louis and Alton. "They must have anticipated violence and it is our belief that had a single one of those papers sternly, firmly, yet soberly depicted the enormity of violence, the blood of Mr. Lovejoy never would have 'cried from the ground.' The *Alton Telegraph*, for instance, has spoken against using violence, but in words so softly that they only seemed an incentive. These remarks will apply with still greater force to the *Missouri Republican*. One of the editors of each of these papers were members of the same religious society with Mr. Lovejoy, and together partook of the same sacrament of the Supper of the Lord. The settlement of their account is with their God, not with us."[40] The next issue of the Galena newspaper indicated that its strong remarks met with considerable opposition among the people. To the credit of the newspaper, it did not back down on its stand.

In addition to the response of the majority of newspaper editors in the country, pastors all over the nation reacted to the slaying of their fellow member of the clergy with emotional, moving appeals, especially on the issue of slavery. In a sermon in New York, one religious leader responded: "Let the ministers of the Gospel who have refused to pray and preach in behalf of their 'countrymen in chains' look to it. Have they not consented to the death of Lovejoy? What are they all but bloody men, who without a word of remonstrance or an effort at resistance, have seen freedom clove down in the broad highway?" He also condemned Illinois, where "a soil professedly consecrated to freedom drank our brother's blood," and Alton: "What is at Alton, at this moment, but the rendezvous of outlaws — the hiding place of confessed murderers?"[41] In Lovejoy's native Maine, Rev. Thomas Stone orated: "The name of our brother is among the few which will never die. It is a name for the world and for all ages. . . . The echo from Europe will be . . . like the voice of ten thousand thunders: proud, boastful Americans! Tell us of your equal rights, your elective franchise; your popular government. Paper constitutions you have indeed; mere waste-paper!"[42] Some antislavery Lovejoy supporters, particularly among the pacifist Friends (Quakers), criticized Lovejoy for defending the printing equipment and firing at the mob. To this, Rev. Chester Hardwick of Hardwick, Vermont, responded: "If I ever assault a family with murderous intent, I would that the head of that family resist me unto blood, if he cannot control me otherwise. . . . If I join a mob to destroy a printing press to stifle free discussion, if I assault the defenders of that press, and attempt to fire the building in which they have intrenched themselves, [then I want] some lover of his country, some bold defender of its sacred liberties, some generous friends of the oppressed and trodden down slave . . . [to] shoot me dead."[43]

Leading citizens added their voices to the national chorus. Horace Greeley, the nation's most prominent journalist and a future presidential candidate, called Lovejoy "a martyr to public liberty" for "the act of inflexibly maintaining the common rights of every citizen."[44] In Springfield, Illinois, soon to be the state capital, silence prevailed on the Lovejoy tragedy, apart from the simple reporting of the event in the newspapers. No editorial commented. But State Representative Abraham Lincoln made a speech about mob rule and its dangers. He carefully avoided mentioning the name of Lovejoy, but everyone knew to whom he referred. Three of those responsible for the mob action—Linder, Hogan, and Edwards—were friends of Lincoln and people with political power. Twenty-eight-year-old Lincoln gave not his first speech but the first speech that would reflect the Lincoln style for the remainder of his life: "Let every man remember that to violate the law, is to trample on the blood of his father, and to tear the charter of his own, and his children's liberty. Let reverence for the laws be breathed by every American mother, to the lisping babe that prattles on her lap. . . . In short, let it become the political religion of the nation; and let the old and the young, the rich and the poor, the grave and the gay, of all sexes and tongues, and colors and conditions, sacrifice unceasingly upon its altars."[45]

Public meetings throughout the North and West, particularly in New England, adopted resolutions condemning the slaying and lauding Lovejoy. Unique was a meeting of the "Coloured Citizens of New York" held in a place described simply as "Rev. Theodore S. Wright's Church." They adopted a resolution condemning the "deliberate and brutal murder of the Rev. Elijah P. Lovejoy, who gave up his life . . . sustaining the liberty of the press and the holy principles of Abolition, to which he was honoured of God to become the first Martyr in this nation. . . . In common with the friends of . . . oppressed humanity of our nation, we . . . express our deep and heartfelt sympathy for his heroic wife . . . and implore the blessing of the god of the oppressed to descend upon her and her dear fatherless children."[46]

Within weeks after Lovejoy's death, membership in antislavery societies multiplied, and antislavery sentiment increased. College students held meetings in Ohio and Maine and other states. Rev. Edward Brown relates this story of an incident at Union College in Ohio:

Prof. Laurens P. Hickok [later President of Union College] was regarded as a conservative on the question of emancipation. One afternoon in November, 1837, we heard a rapid trampling through the college halls. Soon we saw it was Prof. Hickok who entered greatly excited. He said, "I want you all to come down to the old chapel room immediately. I have some very important news."

The room was filled with both faculty and students. Prof. Hickok had brought a paper containing an account of the murder of Lovejoy. After reading it he proposed a meeting at the Congregational church in the village two days later.

The next day he mounted his horse and rode all over the township calling at every house and inviting the people to the meeting. At the meeting he made a most eloquent speech.

John Brown, who had sat silent in the back part of the room, rose, lifting up his right hand and saying, "Here, before God, in the presence of these witnesses, from this time I consecrate my life to the destruction of slavery!"[47]

It was a decision from which he never went back. John Brown became both a prominent and controversial figure in the fight over whether Kansas would be a free or a slave state as well as the center of an emotional storm on the whole slavery issue.

At Illinois College in Jacksonville, where Beecher served as president, one of the students, William Herndon, got caught up in the antislavery feeling that swept the campus after Lovejoy's murder. Herndon's father lived in Springfield and supported slavery. When he saw to what Illinois College had exposed his son, he pulled young Herndon out of the school. "But it was too late," William Herndon wrote. "My soul had absorbed too much of what my father believed was rank poison. The murder of Lovejoy filled me with desperation."[48] At his father's insistence, Herndon left college and returned to Springfield. He took up the practice of law—there were no academic requirements then—and encouraged the antislavery thinking of the man who would be his law partner for life, Abraham Lincoln.

In Belleville, Illinois, thirty miles from Alton, a young attorney named Lyman Trumbull wrote to his father five days after the Lovejoy slaying, describing it as an "awful catastrophe which has caused great excitement throughout this section of the country. Both friends and foes bear testimony to the excellence of Lovejoy's private character. His death and the manner in which he was slain will make thousands of Abolitionists, and far more than his writings would have made had he published his paper a hundred years. This transaction is looked on here as not only a disgrace to Alton, but to the whole state. As much as I am opposed to the immediate emancipation of the slaves and to the doctrine of Abolitionism, yet had I been in Alton, I would have cheerfully marched to the rescue of Mr. Lovejoy and his property."[49] Lyman Trumbull later became a U.S. senator from Illinois and the author of the Thirteenth Amendment to the Constitution, which declared the abolition of slavery "within the United States or any place subject to their jurisdiction." And one of the leading journalists in the antislavery cause, Edmund Quincy, son of Harvard president Josiah Quincy, became an Abolitionist after "the awful catastrophe at Alton. . . . The outrages perpetrated upon Mr. Lovejoy and the liberty of the press at St. Louis and Alton dispelled all doubt of the unparalleled iniquity of holding human beings in the condition of domesticated brutes."[50]

Nevertheless, it should be remembered that proslavery sentiment at the time prevailed not just in the South but in the North as well. Two years before Lovejoy's death, the mayor of Boston saved the antislavery leader William Lloyd Garrison from a mob bent on hanging Garrison only by placing him in jail as "a disturber of the peace." But even though a majority of the nation's population still favored not interfering with slavery, never before had their position been so challenged as by Lovejoy's death.

In Boston, the antislavery people wanted to hold a public

meeting to protest Lovejoy's death. City officials at first refused to let them use Faneuil Hall but finally permitted a morning meeting, figuring not many would be there at that time of day. Promoters billed the meeting as "an expression of public senti- ment in regard to the late ferocious assault on the liberty of the press at Alton." Instead of a small crowd, thousands turned out, filling the hall and overflowing into the street. (It was the first time women were admitted to Faneuil Hall.) The meeting began in an orderly fashion. A leading member of the Boston clergy, Dr. William Ellery Channing, spoke, and then someone presented a resolution condemning the Alton incidents. Suddenly, Attorney General James Austin of Massachusetts stood. He referred to blacks as "wild beasts" and to the mob as men like the patriots who threw the tea overboard in the famed Boston Tea Party. He spoke to a crowd composed both of proslavery and of antislavery people as well as many uncommitted who came for the excite- ment and entertainment, which the attorney general appeared to be providing. Austin claimed that as a minister Lovejoy was "out of place" for becoming involved in the slavery issue and that he had "died as the fool dieth." There were cheers when the attorney general finished his remarks. The antislavery *Liberator* later referred to his speech as "fraught with moral stupidity and sulkiness, and all that is malicious, defamatory, undemocratic and murderous."[51]

Then a young attorney in the audience rose to respond. He had not intended to speak and had no prepared remarks. His name was Wendell Phillips. He was interrupted at first with a mixture of cheers, hisses, and boos, and at one point, it appeared that order could not be restored. But he made his plea so eloquently that one historian has described it as one of the three great speeches in U.S. history. Phillips told the attorney general of Massachusetts that when that official compared the mob to the heroes of the American Revolution, Phillips expected the "earth

should have yawned and swallowed him up."[52] In response to the
attorney general's charge that Lovejoy's actions were imprudent,
Phillips responded: "Imprudent to defend freedom of the press!
Why? Because the defense was unsuccessful? Does success gild
crime into patriotism? . . . From the bottom of my heart I thank
that brave little band at Alton for resisting."[53] By the time
Wendell Phillips finished speaking, he had the crowd with him,
and he soon became one of the two major leaders of the
antislavery movement in the nation. Phillips had spoken only
once before on the subject of slavery, before the small Lynn,
Massachusetts, chapter of the Antislavery Society. One observer
present at the Boston meeting wrote that he "had never heard
words there or elsewhere that so thrilled me with the majesty of
true eloquence."[54]

This national response to the Lovejoy murder continued even
after the immediate shock of his death. Two months after the
slaying, a Rochester, New York, writer observed: "Nothing has
happened in many years which has produced so electric an effect
upon the public mind as this."[55] Three months after the death of
Lovejoy, his brother Owen wrote on stationery with a sketch of a
slave being freed. Above the picture of the slave were these
words: "Lovejoy, The First Martyr to American Liberty. Murdered For Asserting The Freedom Of The Press, Alton, Nov. 7,
1837."[56] Antislavery organizations used the same stationery. In
1838, two of Lovejoy's brothers, Joseph and Owen, also published a small book, *Memoir*, about the martyr. Seventeen years
after Lovejoy's death, perhaps predictably, former Illinois Governor Thomas Ford, whose term followed the tragedy, wrote:
"This affair has made a great noise in the world."[57] The
governor reflected the thinking of many, even in 1854: "No
language can be loaded with sufficient severity for the fanatical
leaders [Lovejoy and Beecher] who . . . by their utter disregard
of honest prejudices, drove a peaceful community to a temporary

insanity, and to the commission of enormous crimes."[58] But John Quincy Adams, former president of the United States, wrote later that Lovejoy's death was "a shock as of an earthquake throughout the continent."[59] And Ralph Waldo Emerson paid tribute to "the brave Lovejoy [who] gave his breast to the bullets of a mob, and died when it was better not to live."[60]

Fortunately, some animosities die. Five years after Lovejoy's slaying, the catalog for the school founded by Benjamin Godfrey, Monticello Female Seminary, listed as its trustees some of those on both sides of the Lovejoy controversy, including Winthrop Gilman and Cyrus Edwards.[61]

The bad reputation of Alton died slowly, much too late for the city ever to regain its prominent position in the Midwest. By the time people had forgotten the Lovejoy incident, the population centers were established. Twenty-three years following the murder of Lovejoy, an Alton resident traveled to Cincinnati, and when he told the person with whom he spoke where he lived, the response came back vigorously: "Alton! It is covered with blood!"[62] Two years after the end of the Civil War, Wendell Phillips wrote: "Up to this time the name of Alton has always brought one idea to my mind and I never hear its name or see it printed without an involuntary shudder."[63] Phillips made his comments about Alton when he visited the town and the key Lovejoy scenes. From Alton he wrote to the *Anti-Slavery Standard* describing Lovejoy's death as one that "stunned a drunken people into sobriety." He added: "I can never forget the quick, sharp agony of that hour which brought us the news of Lovejoy's death. We had not then fully learned the bloodthirstiness of the slave power. The gun fired at Lovejoy was like that of Sumter—it shattered a world of dreams." Phillips concluded with these memorable words: "How prudently most men creep into nameless graves while now and then one or two forget themselves into immortality."[64]

From a vantage point of forty-four years, another author wrote: "It is difficult for the present generation to realize the intensity of the excitement that was produced forty years ago by the death of this brave man."[65] A writer in 1900, sixty-three years after Lovejoy's death, told of being a boy when the slaying of Lovejoy occurred, and he described it as "like the shot heard round the world at Concord Bridge."[66]

Lovejoy's birthplace, Albion, Maine, is now a small village struggling to survive. Lovejoy Pond is still known to the people in the area as Lovejoy Pond. Some years ago, faculty from Colby College erected a small sign, now in disrepair, at the site of his home. As late as 1923, a local minister wrote that some of the stone and the chimney of the home were visible, but that is no longer true.[67] There is a Lovejoy family cemetery, approximately twenty feet square, with a number of markers. One of the few gravestones that is still legible notes the death of Lovejoy's father, Rev. Daniel Lovejoy, August 11, 1833. In 1957, the town of Albion donated to Colby College the cemetery and the land on which the Lovejoy home once stood. In the community is a small facility known as the Lovejoy Health Center. And townspeople speak of Elijah Lovejoy with great pride.

For many years, Lovejoy's grave was marked by a simple pine board with the letters *E.P.L.* carved onto it, but eventually even this disappeared. Then a citizen named Thomas Dimmock traced the spot where Lovejoy was buried. A road in the Alton City Cemetery had gone over it. Dimmock felt that Lovejoy deserved better recognition, and at his own expense, he had the body removed and a small marble tablet placed at the new grave engraved with the words (written in Latin): "Here lies Lovejoy. Spare him now that he is buried." Largely through the promptings of Thomas Dimmock, the citizens of Alton recognized that something more appropriate should be done, and in 1897, they erected a large, suitable monument, which still stands. At the dedication of the monument in 1897, one of the speakers was Rev. J. M. Wilkerson, pastor of the African Methodist Episcopal Church in Alton. Elijah Lovejoy would have applauded his words: "I am unlike many of my race, who are constantly trying to apologize for being black. I have never felt it to be necessary for me to apologize for God Almighty. If He, in His great wisdom, saw fit to make me a black man, and another a white man, that is none of my business, neither is it yours. Those who think that God made some mistake about the matter, I refer them to Him for settlement of the matter and not me."[68]

🕊 Postscript

The historical importance of Lovejoy's death does not need elaboration, but the battles he fought are never completely won. However trite it may sound, eternal vigilance really is the price of liberty. If we view Lovejoy's life simply as an act on the stage of history, an act that we have applauded but that now is finished, then this volume has too little meaning. Lovejoy's life and death should help us look to the future as well as to history. A few conclusions can be ventured, conclusions that while obvious to the reader are less apparent to many of our fellow citizens.

The people who really killed Lovejoy were not those who fired the bullets but rather "middle of the road" straddlers, most of them honorable people in the community. They were all the clean, decent, honest people who stayed neutral between the two opposing forces and who were too timid to stand and be counted. They were the people who said they "could see both sides to the question," who did nothing, and who were thereby guilty of a spinelessness that resulted in Lovejoy's death. They made it possible for others to aim the guns and pull the triggers.

A few days before his death, Lovejoy wrote to the *Liberator*: "The pulpit, with one exception, is silent. Brother Graves was absent about the time of the first outrage. . . . We have a few excellent brethren here in Alton. They are sincerely desirous to know their duty in this crisis, and to do it. But as yet, they cannot see that duty requires them to maintain their cause here at all hazards."[1]

There are times when decisions may be difficult and when there may be no reason to take a position. But there are also times, like this one, when to be neutral in a fight between right and wrong is to be on the side of the wrong. "Middle of the road" Germans stood silently while Hitler butchered the Jews. Contrast that with Denmark, where the clergy and others stood up to the Nazis and became the only occupied country to rescue almost all of its Jewish population. From a Birmingham jail, Martin Luther King, Jr., wrote: "I have almost reached the regrettable conclusion that the Negro's great stumbling block in his stride toward freedom is not the White Citizens' Counciler or the Ku Klux Klanner, but the white moderate who is more devoted to 'order' than to justice, who prefers a negative peace which is the absence of tension to a positive peace which is the presence of justice."[2] There are times when right is right and wrong is wrong—when you have to stand up, even though it may be unpopular. Had Lincoln taken a poll, he never would have issued his then-unpopular Emancipation Proclamation.

Interestingly enough, almost half the men who gathered in the Gilman warehouse that fatal night were in business. They stood to lose much at the hands of an unhappy public, but they still firmly supported basic freedoms. The best example is Winthrop Gilman, who risked everything. Yet I know businesspeople, teachers, and preachers (Lovejoy was all three) who are even afraid to ask for a party primary ballot for fear it might "offend" someone.

As the demand for courageous action grows, the numbers willing to take action shrinks. Those who do a coward's toe dance through life may please the immediate audience, but history acclaims those who are willing to march for their beliefs, even though the terrain may be rough and there will be missteps.

Lovejoy was not by nature a giant of a man, not by nature a crusader. He simply had certain beliefs, stuck with them, and changed history. Listen to what Samuel Willard, one of the men who knew Lovejoy in Alton, said: "No man seemed less fitted to stand foremost in a great struggle. . . . Mr. Lovejoy was a gentle man always. His firmness was not that of passion and obstinacy, but the gentle persistence of one who felt that he was right. There was no bitterness in his heart, no venom in his tongue, no sound of fury in his voice."[3]

In reading the works of history that glorify the actions of historical figures, it is easy to forget that these are people like you and me. Some, like Thomas Jefferson, are persons of outstanding ability, but the majority are not. Most changes in history are not made by intellectual giants who sweep across the pages of our history books but rather by people who do not seem "fitted to stand foremost in a great struggle"; they simply have certain beliefs and are willing patiently but firmly and courageously to support them.

Lovejoy's fight was a struggle to make his faith something more than a repetition of words. Religion to him was more than well-placed bricks and stained-glass windows. Conventional Christianity or Judaism, which hears comforting sermons but does not wish to disturb, would have no ally in Elijah Lovejoy.

Lovejoy's death does not mark the only battle for freedom lost in Madison County, Illinois. During World War I, rumors spread that Robert Prager, a coal miner from Collinsville, Illinois, was a spy. Born in Dresden, Germany, he spoke only German. When a mob formed to seize him, he could not speak English to defend himself, and they quickly hanged this completely innocent man.

These two murders stand out, but there have been many less dramatic defeats, and Madison County is perhaps not different from the county and community in which you who read this live. Defeats occur in every community in every state. Whether we are able to hold the number of such defeats to a minimum will determine whether the freedom for which Lovejoy died will survive. He understood that the struggle for freedom is never ending. Freedom in a community dies a little when public officials are willing to take money for votes or favors; freedom is diminished when school boards and city councils hold secret meetings, keeping out the public who elected them; freedom is eroded when law enforcement officials want to stop crime by using methods that violate freedoms given to us in our Constitution; freedom suffers a defeat when a teacher or a member of the clergy or anyone in a community is not permitted to express an unpopular opinion. And freedom is set back when any citizen does not have an equal opportunity for a job. Because the battle will always go on, there must be citizens who are willing to match each defeat with a victory.

Lovejoy's fight was a struggle for dignity and opportunity for the oppressed. We are in a world filled with the oppressed. Some lack freedom. Some lack food. Some are disabled and treated worse than cattle. Some lack the ability to get a job because of the color of their skin, their national background, their religious beliefs, or their sexual orientation.

We now increasingly stockpile the poor into central cities and then reduce the resources available to cities to deal with their problems. While racial integration has gradually improved in the nation, economic integration has declined. We now put people who do not know how to solve their problems next to people who do not know how to solve their problems and thereby compound the problems. That is a fairly dramatic change in our residential pattern. Unless you live in a small community, the people who live in your neighborhood are probably of an economic status similar to your own. And because the problems of the struggling are more distant, it has become easy for middle-income and wealthier Americans to ignore the poor, or worse, to condemn them, while a declining percentage of the U.S. tax dollar goes to help the poor both in our country and in other nations.

There is no scarcity of people who are oppressed. There is only a scarcity of men and women with eyes clear enough to see and hearts big enough to act.

❧ Notes

Index

Notes

1. From Maine to the Frontier

1. Rev. Thomas Adams, eulogy for Daniel Lovejoy, quoted in Joseph C. Lovejoy and Owen Lovejoy, *Memoir of the Rev. Elijah P. Lovejoy* (New York: John Taylor, 1838), 14.

2. Daniel Lovejoy to Elijah Lovejoy, letter, Mar. 19, 1832, *Memoir*, 44.

3. Elijah Lovejoy to Sybil Lovejoy, letter, Apr. 24, 1832, *Memoir*, 49.

4. Daniel Lovejoy, memorandum, Feb. 1831(?), undated, Wickett-Wiswall Collection of Lovejoy Papers, Southwest Collection, Texas Technological University, Lubbock, Texas.

5. Rev. Thomas Adams, eulogy for Daniel Lovejoy, *Memoir*, 15.

6. Elijah Lovejoy to Daniel Lovejoy, letter, undated, Wickett-Wiswall Collection.

7. Society for the Propagating of the Gospel among the Indians, to Rev. Daniel Lovejoy, June 1, 1807, Wickett-Wiswall Collection.

8. Elijah Lovejoy to Sybil Lovejoy, letter, Apr. 24, 1832, Wickett-Wiswall Collection.

9. Samuel Willard, quoted in Henry Tanner, *The Martyrdom of Lovejoy* (Chicago: Fergus Printing, 1881; New York: Augustus Kelley Publishers, 1971), 216.

10. Elijah Lovejoy to Elizabeth Lovejoy, letter, Sept. 24, 1824, Wickett-Wiswall Collection.

11. Elizabeth Lovejoy to Elijah Lovejoy, letter, May 10, 1822, Wickett-Wiswall Collection.

12. Daniel Lovejoy to Elijah Lovejoy, letter, July 31, 1824, Wickett-Wiswall Collection.

13. Elijah Lovejoy to Daniel Lovejoy, letter, Sept. 26, 1824, Wickett-Wiswall Collection.

14. Elijah Lovejoy, commencement address, Waterville College, 1826, Wickett-Wiswall Collection.

15. Elijah Lovejoy, poem, *Memoir*, 29–31.

16. Elijah Lovejoy, poem, *Memoir*, 31.

17. Elijah Lovejoy, diary, May 19, 1827, Special Collections, Miller Library, Colby College, Waterville, Maine.

18. Elijah Lovejoy, diary, May 19, 1827, Special Collections, Miller Library.

19. Signed "Viator" but written by Elijah Lovejoy to Rev. Cook, Ware, Massachusetts, letter, June 4, 1827, diary, Special Collections, Miller Library.

20. Elijah Lovejoy, diary, Special Collections, Miller Library.

21. Elijah Lovejoy, diary, quoted in *Memoir*, 31.

22. Elijah Lovejoy to Daniel and Elizabeth Lovejoy, letter, Mar. 15, 1829, Wickett-Wiswall Collection.

23. Elizabeth Lovejoy to Elijah Lovejoy, letter, Apr. 27, 1829, Wickett-Wiswall Collection.

24. Elijah Lovejoy to Daniel and Elizabeth Lovejoy, letter, Mar. 15, 1829, Wickett-Wiswall Collection.

25. Elizabeth Lovejoy to Elijah Lovejoy, letter, Apr. 27, 1829, Wickett-Wiswall Collection.

26. Elijah Lovejoy, poem, *Memoir*, 37.

27. *St. Louis Beacon*, Oct. 14, 1830.

28. *Richmond Enquirer*, quoted in *St. Louis Times*, June 4, 1831.

29. Elijah Lovejoy to Daniel and Elizabeth Lovejoy, letter, Mar. 15, 1829, Wickett-Wiswall Collection.

30. *St. Louis Times*, Aug. 28, 1830.

31. *St. Louis Times*, Oct. 9, 1830.

32. *St. Louis Times*, Aug. 21, 1830.

33. *St. Louis Times*, Aug. 21, 1830.

34. *St. Louis Times*, June 11, 1831.

35. *St. Louis Times*, Aug. 27, 1831.

36. *St. Louis Times*, Sept. 3, 1831.

37. *St. Louis Times*, Jan. 14, 1832.

38. *St. Louis Times*, Jan. 15, 1831; Feb. 19, 1831; Apr. 2, 1831; Sept. 4, 1830; Sept. 25, 1830; Nov. 27, 1830; July 23, 1831; Aug. 13, 1831; Jan. 14, 1832; Apr. 9, 1831.

39. *St. Louis Times*, Jan. 7, 1832.

40. William Wells Brown, *Illustrated Edition of the Life and Escape of Wm. Wells Brown from American Slavery* (Boston: Anti-Slavery Society, 1847), 26–29.

2.   Editor, Preacher, and Fighter

1. *St. Louis Times*, Apr. 9, 1831.
2. Elijah Lovejoy to Daniel and Elizabeth Lovejoy, letter, Feb. 1831, *Memoir*, 39.
3. Elijah Lovejoy to Daniel and Elizabeth Lovejoy, letter, *Memoir*, 41–43.
4. Elizabeth Lovejoy to Elijah Lovejoy, letter, Mar. 19, 1832, Wickett-Wiswall Collection.
5. Daniel Lovejoy to Elijah Lovejoy, letter, Mar. 19, 1832, Wickett-Wiswall Collection.
6. Joseph Lovejoy to Daniel and Elizabeth Lovejoy, letter, Mar. 1, 1832, Wickett-Wiswall Collection.
7. Elijah Lovejoy to Sybil Lovejoy, letter, Apr. 24, 1832, Wickett-Wiswall Collection.
8. Elijah Lovejoy to Joseph Lovejoy, letter, Feb. 12, 1833, Chicago Historical Society Library manuscript.
9. Elijah Lovejoy to Daniel and Elizabeth Lovejoy, letter, Aug. 5, 1833, Wickett-Wiswall Collection.
10. Elijah Lovejoy to Owen Lovejoy, letter, Aug. 26, 1833, Wickett-Wiswall Collection.
11. Elijah Lovejoy to Elizabeth Lovejoy, letter, Oct. 21, 1833, Chicago Historical Society Library manuscript.
12. Headings, St. Louis *Observer*, Jan. 2, 1834.
13. *Philadelphian*, quoted in St. Louis *Observer*, Jan. 9, 1834.
14. St. Louis *Observer*, Sept. 3, 1835.
15. St. Louis *Observer*, Jan. 16, 1834; Jan. 30, 1834; Jan. 30, 1834; Feb. 13, 1834; Nov. 13, 1834; Mar. 6, 1834; Oct. 16, 1834.
16. Elijah Lovejoy to Rev. John Brooks, letter, May 1, 1834, Chicago Historical Society Library manuscript.
17. St. Louis *Observer*, May 22, 1834.
18. St. Louis *Observer*, Oct. 16, 1834.
19. St. Louis *Observer*, Nov. 13, 1834.

20. St. Louis *Observer*, Nov. 6, 1834.

21. Elijah Lovejoy to Rev. John Brooks, letter, Dec. 26, 1833, Chicago Historical Society Library manuscript.

22. St. Louis *Observer*, Dec. 11, 1834.

23. St. Louis *Observer*, June 19, 1834.

24. St. Louis *Observer*, Sept. 4, 1834.

25. St. Louis *Observer*, Apr. 16, 1835.

26. St. Louis *Observer*, Apr. 30, 1835.

27. St. Louis *Observer*, July 31, 1834.

28. St. Louis *Observer*, Feb. 13, 1834.

29. St. Louis *Observer*, May 21, 1835.

30. St. Louis *Observer*, Nov. 27, 1834.

31. St. Louis *Observer*, May 21, 1835.

32. St. Louis *Observer*, July 31, 1834.

33. St. Louis *Observer*, Aug. 21, 1834.

34. St. Louis *Observer*, May 15, 1834.

35. Elijah Lovejoy to Joseph Lovejoy, letter, Nov. 21, 1834, Wickett-Wiswall Collection.

36. St. Louis *Observer*, Aug. 21, 1834.

37. St. Louis *Observer*, Aug. 24, 1834.

38. St. Louis *Observer*, Nov. 27, 1834.

39. Elijah Lovejoy to Elizabeth Lovejoy, letter, *Memoir*, 133–34.

40. St. Louis *Observer*, Sept. 10, 1835.

41. Elijah Lovejoy to Joseph Lovejoy, letter, Jan. 1836, *Memoir*, 161.

42. St. Louis *Observer*, Nov. 5, 1835.

43. Samuel G. Hart to Elijah Lovejoy, letter, Sept. 8, 1835, Wickett-Wiswall Collection.

44. *St. Louis Commercial Bulletin*, Oct. 21, 1835.

45. St. Louis *Observer*, Nov. 5, 1835.

46. Elijah Lovejoy to Elizabeth Lovejoy, letter, Nov. 23, 1835, Wickett-Wiswall Collection.

47. Elijah Lovejoy to Garritt Smith, letter, Nov. 20, 1835, Chicago Historical Society Library Papers.

48. *Missouri Republican*, Nov. 7, 1835.

49. Elijah Lovejoy to Joseph Lovejoy, letter, Jan. 1836, undated, Wickett-Wiswall Collection.

50. Elijah Lovejoy to Joseph Lovejoy, letter, Jan. 1836, undated,

Wickett-Wiswall Collection.

51. St. Louis *Observer*, Oct. 8, 1835.

52. St. Louis *Observer*, Oct. 22, 1835.

53. St. Louis *Observer*, Nov. 5, 1835. Lovejoy quotations are from the *Observer* in the same and several succeeding issues.

54. St. Louis *Observer*, Nov. 5, 1835.

55. St. Louis *Observer*, Nov. 5, 1835.

56. St. Louis *Observer*, Nov. 5, 1835.

57. St. Louis *Observer*, Nov. 5, 1835.

58. St. Louis *Observer*, Dec. 17, 1835.

59. Elijah Lovejoy to unnamed brother, letter, Nov. 2, 1835, *Memoir*, 155–56.

3.   A Horrible Murder

1. Elijah Lovejoy to Elizabeth Lovejoy, letter, Nov. 23, 1835, *Memoir*, 158–59.

2. Handbill and *Missouri Republican*, quoted in St. Louis *Observer*, Dec. 10, 1835.

3. St. Louis *Observer*, Dec. 3, 1835.

4. St. Louis *Observer*, Nov. 19, 1835.

5. Edward Beecher to Elijah Lovejoy, letter, Dec. 20, 1835, Wickett-Wiswall Collection.

6. St. Louis *Observer*, Dec. 31, 1835.

7. *Alton Telegraph*, Mar. 30, 1836.

8. The details of the murder scene are based on accounts from the St. Louis *Observer* (May 5, 1836) and the other St. Louis newspapers, the *Missouri Republican* and the *Missouri Argus*.

9. St. Louis *Observer*, May 5, 1836.

10. *Missouri Republican*, Apr. 30, 1836.

11. St. Louis *Observer*, May 5, 1836.

12. *Missouri Republican*, Apr. 30, 1836; *Missouri Argus*, Apr. 29, 1836.

13. Recollections of Captain Dillon, *Cincinnati Enquirer*, undated, quoted in John Gill, *Tide Without Turning* (Boston: Starr King Press, 1958), 61.

14. St. Louis *Observer*, May 5, 1836.

15. St. Louis *Observer*, May 5, 1836.

16. *Missouri Republican*, May 12, 1836.

17. Abraham Lincoln, *Collected Works of Abraham Lincoln*, ed. Roy P. Basler, vol. 1, (New Brunswick, N.J.: Rutgers Univ. Press, 1953), 108–15.

18. John Lovejoy to Elizabeth Lovejoy, letter, Apr. 30, 1836, Wickett-Wiswall Collection.

19. *Illinois State Register and Illinois Advocate*, May 6, 1836.

20. *Illinois State Register and Illinois Advocate*, May 13, 1836.

21. *Missouri Republican*, May 3, 1836.

22. *Emancipator*, June 30, 1836.

23. St. Louis *Observer*, May 12, 1836.

24. St. Louis *Observer*, June 2, 1836.

25. St. Louis *Observer*, June 9, 1836.

26. St. Louis *Observer*, July 14, 1836.

27. *Missouri Republican*, Jan. 30, 1835.

28. *Missouri Republican*, Sept. 12, 1835.

29. *Missouri Republican*, May 26, 1836. Judge Lawless's outrageous comments are similar to those of a Springfield, Illinois, newspaper after the race riots there in 1908: "The implication is clear that conditions, not the populace, were to blame and that many good citizens could find no other remedy than that applied by the mob. It was not the face of the whites' hatred toward the negroes, but of the negroes' own misconduct, general inferiority or unfitness for free institutions that were at fault" (*Illinois State Journal*, Aug. 15–16, 1908, quoted in Roberta Senechal, *Sociogenesis of a Race Riot* [Urbana: Univ. of Illinois Press, 1990], 42).

30. St. Louis *Observer*, July 21, 1836.

31. *Missouri Republican*, May 26, 1836.

32. *Missouri Republican*, May 26, 1836.

33. Newspaper quotations are from the St. Louis *Observer*, May 12, 1836; May 19, 1836; May 26, 1836.

34. *Emancipator*, Aug. 4, 1836.

35. St. Louis *Observer*, July 21, 1836; May 26, 1836.

36. *Missouri Republican*, May 5, 1836.

37. Elizabeth Lovejoy to Owen Lovejoy, letter, Sept. 28, 1837, Lovejoy Papers, William L. Clements Library, University of Michigan, Ann Arbor, Michigan.

38. St. Louis *Observer*, Nov. 5, 1835.

39. *Shepherd of the Valley*, Feb. 21, 1834, quoted in "Elijah P. Lovejoy as an Anti-Catholic," *Records of the American Catholic Historical Society of Philadelphia*, Sept. 1951.

40. *Shepherd of the Valley*, June 13, 1835.

41. Both the publication of Maria Monk's *Awful Disclosures* and the Stanton observation are discussed briefly by Sen. Daniel Patrick Moynihan in his book *Pandaemonium* (New York: Oxford Univ. Press, 1993), 31.

42. St. Louis *Observer*, June 21, 1836.

43. *Missouri Republican*, July 23, 1836.

44. John Lovejoy to Elizabeth Lovejoy, letter, July 26, 1836, Wickett-Wiswall Collection.

45. Elijah Lovejoy to Elizabeth Lovejoy, letter, quoted in Tanner, *Martyrdom*, 89, 90.

46. Joseph Brown, "Early Reminiscences of Alton," lecture, Feb. 21, 1896, Special Collections, Miller Library.

47. Edward Magdol, *Owen Lovejoy: Abolitionist in Congress* (New Brunswick, N.J.: Rutgers Univ. Press, 1967), 13.

48. *Alton Telegraph*, Sept. 21, 1836.

49. Alton *Observer*, Dec. 15, 1836.

50. Alton *Observer*, Nov. 3, 1836.

4.   A Press in the River

1. Gallatin County Records, quoted in John W. Allen, *Legends and Lore of Southern Illinois* (Carbondale: Southern Illinois Univ. Press, 1963), 256.

2. "Will of Shadrach Bond, First Governor of Illinois, Under Statehood. Found in the County Clerk's Office of Randolph County," *Illinois State Historical Society Journal*, Apr. 1927.

3. John W. Allen, "Slavery and Negro Servitude in Pope County, Illinois," *Illinois State Historical Society Journal*, Dec. 1949.

4. Joseph Brown, "Early Reminiscences of Alton," lecture, Feb. 21, 1896, Special Collections, Miller Library.

5. Harvey Reid, *Enoch Long, An Illinois Pioneer* (Chicago: Fergus Printing, 1884), 70–71.

6. Thomas Dimmock, "Lovejoy," address, Mar. 14, 1888, Illinois State Historical Library, Springfield, Illinois, 10–11.

7. *Alton Telegraph*, Aug. 10, 1836.

8. John Lovejoy to Elizabeth Lovejoy, letter, Sept. 4, 1836, Wickett-Wiswall Collection.

9. Alton *Observer*, Apr. 6, 1837.

10. J. M., "Viscount Melbourne," Alton *Observer*, Sept. 8, 1836.

11. Alton *Observer*, May 25, 1837.

12. Alton *Observer*, Jan. 5, 1837.

13. Alton *Observer*, Sept. 29, 1836.

14. Elijah Lovejoy to Elizabeth Lovejoy, letter, Aug. 31, 1836, Chicago Historical Society Library Papers.

15. John Lovejoy to Elizabeth Lovejoy, letter, Apr. 30, 1836, Wickett-Wiswall Collection.

16. Elijah Lovejoy to Elizabeth Lovejoy, letter, Apr. 14, 1837, Wickett-Wiswall Collection.

17. John Lovejoy to Elizabeth Lovejoy, letter, Apr. 30, 1836, Wickett-Wiswall Collection.

18. Alton *Observer*, Nov. 3, 1836.

19. Alton *Observer*, Mar. 10, 1837.

20. Joseph Brown, "Early Reminiscences of Alton," lecture, Feb. 21, 1896, Special Collections, Miller Library.

21. Alton *Observer*, Jan. 26, 1837.

22. Alton *Observer*, Feb. 2, 1837.

23. Alton *Observer*, Jan. 26, 1837.

24. *Missouri Republican*, Feb. 15, 1837.

25. *Missouri Republican*, Feb. 7, 1837.

26. Alton *Observer*, Jan. 12, 1837.

27. Alton *Observer*, Feb. 2, 1837.

28. Alton *Observer*, Feb. 9, 1837.

29. Elijah Lovejoy to Major G. C. Sibley, letter, Apr. 27, 1837, Missouri Historical Society Library, St. Louis, Missouri.

30. Major G. C. Sibley to Elijah Lovejoy, letter, June 12, 1837, Missouri Historical Society Library.

31. Edward Beecher, *Narrative of Riots at Alton* (Alton: George Holton, 1838), 20.

5.   Danger and Violence

1. Alton *Observer*, July 6, 1837.
2. Elizabeth Lovejoy to Elijah Lovejoy, letter, 1837, undated, Wickett-Wiswall Collection.
3. Elijah Lovejoy to Joseph Lovejoy, letter, Apr. 14, 1837, Wickett-Wiswall Collection.
4. Alton *Observer*, Mar. 9, 1837.
5. Alton *Observer*, Mar. 16, 1837.
6. Alton *Observer*, July 13, 1837.
7. Alton *Observer*, July 6, 1837.
8. Alton *Observer*, Apr. 13, 1837.
9. *Alton Telegraph*, July 19, 1837.
10. Alton *Observer*, July 20, 1837. Lovejoy printed both the proceedings of the meeting and his reply.
11. *Missouri Republican*, July 17, 1837.
12. Alton *Observer*, July 20, 1837.
13. Alton *Observer*, June 29, 1836.
14. Alton *Observer*, July 20, 1837.
15. *Baptist Banner*, quoted in Alton *Observer*, May 4, 1837.
16. Alton *Observer*, May 4, 1837.
17. Elijah Lovejoy to Rev. Asa Cummings, letter, Feb. 9, 1837, *Memoir*, 192–200.
18. *Memoir*, Mar. 16, 1837, 205.
19. *Memoir*, Mar. 16, 1837, 232–34.
20. *Missouri Republican*, July 17, 1837.
21. *Missouri Republican*, Aug. 17, 1837.
22. *Missouri Republican*, Aug. 22, 1837.
23. *Peoria Register and North-Western Gazetteer*, Sept. 2, 1837.
24. *Missouri Republican*, Aug. 25, 1837.
25. *Missouri Argus*, Aug. 29, 1837.
26. *Alton Telegraph*, quoted in *Illinois State Register and Illinois Advocate*, Sept. 8, 1837.
27. *Alton Telegraph*, Oct. 11, 1837.
28. *Alton Telegraph*, Oct. 11, 1837.
29. Alton *Observer*, July 20, 1837.
30. Isaac Gallard to Elijah Lovejoy, letter, Oct. 5, 1837, Wickett-Wiswall Collection.

31. Alton *Observer*, May 4, 1837.

32. *Memoir*, 245.

33. Elijah Lovejoy to Lewis Tappan and others, letters, Sept. 11, 1837, Library of Congress.

34. *Alton Telegraph*, quoted in *Illinois State Register and Illinois Advocate*, Oct. 6, 1837.

35. *Illinois State Register and Illinois Advocate*, Oct. 6, 1837.

36. *Northwestern Gazette and Galena Advertiser*, Sept. 9, 1837.

37. *Western Adventurer*, quoted in *Emancipator*, Oct. 26, 1837.

38. *Missouri Republican*, Sept. 25, 1837 (incorrectly dated Sept. 26, 1837).

39. *Alton Telegraph*, Sept. 27, 1837.

40. The St. Charles incident is recorded in *Memoir*, 251–60.

41. *Missouri Republican*, Oct. 4, 1837.

6.   Prelude to Death

1. Frank J. Heinl, "Elijah Parish Lovejoy," address, Jacksonville Rotary Club, undated, *Illinois College Alumni Quarterly*, Miller Library.

2. Quoted in Dwight Harris, *The History of Negro Servitude in Illinois* (New York: A. C. McClurg, 1904; New York: Negro Univ. Press, 1969), 80.

3. Alton *Observer*, July 6, 1837.

4. Reid, 86n.

5. Elijah Lovejoy to Gerritt Smith, letter, Sept. 4, 1837, Special Collections, Miller Library.

6. Beecher, 25–27.

7. Beecher, 28.

8. *Missouri Republican*, quoted in *Backwoodsman*, Nov. 3, 1837.

9. *Memoir*, 138.

10. W. T. Norton, "Hon. Robert Smith, Forgotten Statesman of Illinois," *Illinois State Historical Society Journal*, Oct. 1915, 428.

11. Tanner, *Martyrdom*, 109.

12. *Alton Telegraph*, Oct. 25, 1837.

13. *Lynn Record*, quoted in *Emancipator*, Oct. 26, 1837.

14. *Emancipator*, Oct. 26, 1837.

15. Beecher, 28–29.

16. *Illinois State Anti-Slavery Society Minute Book, 1837–44*, Chicago Historical Society.

17. Samuel Willard, quoted in Tanner, *Martyrdom*, 220.

18. *Missouri Republican*, Oct. 30, 1837.

19. *Missouri Republican*, Oct. 30, 1837.

20. *Alton Telegraph*, Nov. 1, 1837.

21. *Missouri Republican*, Nov. 1, 1837.

22. Quotation from Hogan and detailed account of the meeting, *Missouri Republican*, Nov. 10, 1837.

23. Official minutes of the meeting, *Alton Telegraph*, Nov. 8, 1837.

24. Beecher, 60.

25. Beecher, 65.

26. Official minutes of the meeting, *Alton Telegraph*, Nov. 8, 1837.

27. Official minutes of the meeting, quoted in Tanner, *Martyrdom*, 203.

28. Lovejoy's speech is quoted in Beecher, 85–91. After the meeting, Lovejoy and Beecher went home together, and as accurately as possible, they tried to recall what Lovejoy had said and then wrote it down.

29. Benjamin K. Hart, quoted in Thomas Dimmock, "Lovejoy— Hero and Martyr," *New England Magazine*, May 1891.

30. *Memoir*, 275.

31. Official minutes of the meeting, quoted in Tanner, *Martyrdom*, 203.

32. *Peoria Register and North-Western Gazatteer*, Dec. 16, 1837.

33. *Missouri Republican*, Nov. 3, 1837.

34. Beecher, 141–44.

7.   Death

1. John Krum, quoted in *Memoir*, 373.

2. Beecher, 100.

3. Beecher, 101–3.

4. Beecher, 103.

5. J. W. Harned, interview, *Greenville Advocate*, 1898, undated, Illinois State Historical Library.

6. J. W. Harned, interview, *Greenville Advocate*, 1898, undated,

Illinois State Historical Library.

7. Joseph Greeley, quoted in *Alton Trials*, recorded by William S. Lincoln (New York: John F. Trow, Univ. Press, 1838; Arno Press and the *New York Times*, 1970), 22.

8. This quotation and all quotations not otherwise attributed in the remainder of this chapter and in chapter 8 are from the court proceedings as recorded in *Alton Trials*, referred to earlier. At the trials, many of the people involved testified under oath as to what happened. Fortunately, this was recorded by a court reporter.

9. Henry Tanner, *History of the Rise and Progress of the Alton Riots* (Buffalo: James D. Warren, 1878), 10.

10. Tanner, *History*, 11.

11. Samuel Willard, quoted in Tanner, *History*, 226.

12. John Krum, quoted in *Memoir*, 376.

13. *Cincinnati Journal*, quoted in *Liberator*, Dec. 22, 1837.

14. William Martin, quoted in *Alton Trials*, 22.

15. *Memoir*, 291.

16. Reid, 100.

17. *Memoir*, 293.

18. Henry West, quoted in *Alton Trials*, 97.

19. Samuel Willard, quoted in Tanner, *History*, 225.

20. Samuel Thompson, quoted in *Alton Trials*, 47.

21. *Peoria Register and North-Western Gazetteer*, Nov. 11, 1837.

22. *Memoir*, 291–92.

23. *Memoir*, 291–92.

24. Major Clarence E. Lovejoy (self-described historian and genealogist of the Lovejoy family), radio address, WXAL, Boston, Nov. 7, 1937, Special Collections, Miller Library.

25. M. K. Whittlesey, "Elijah P. Lovejoy," *Magazine of Western History*, July 1887.

8. Injustice and Aftermath

1. Winthrop Gilman, quoted in G. L. Ward to Owen Lovejoy, letter, Jan. 14, 1838, Lovejoy Papers, William L. Clements Library.

2. Tanner, *Martyrdom*, 188–89.

3. Section 117, Illinois Revised Statutes of 1837.

4. B. F. Murdock, quoted in *Alton Trials*, 51.

5. G. L. Ward to Owen Lovejoy, letter, Jan. 14, 1838, Lovejoy Papers, William L. Clements Library.

6. Asa Turner, Jr., to Owen Lovejoy, letter, Nov. 6, 1837, Lovejoy Papers, William L. Clements Library.

7. Usher F. Linder, *Reminiscences of the Early Bench and Bar of Illinois* (Chicago: Legal News, 1876), 223, 372.

8. *Lynn Record*, quoted in *Memoir*, 332.

9. Whittlesey.

10. Stephen A. Douglas, quoted in several newspapers in Paul Angle, *Created Equal* (Chicago: Univ. of Chicago Press, 1858), 362.

11. W. T. Norton, *Centennial History of Madison County*, vol. 1 (Chicago, 1912), 387.

12. G. L. Ward to Owen Lovejoy, letter, Jan. 14, 1838, Lovejoy Papers, William L. Clements Library (spelled "Morss" in the letter).

13. Reported to Paul Simon in a 1992 letter from Robert Tabscott, a respected Lovejoy historian. The Wayne County Clerk sent a form letter, in response to an inquiry from Paul Simon, stating that they do not have records going back to that date.

14. Petition of Royal Weller to Henry K. Eaton, Probate Justice of Madison County, Illinois, Feb. 28, 1848, Burton Bernard Papers, Lovejoy Library, Southern Illinois University, Edwardsville, Illinois.

15. Document filed by Owen Lovejoy in Bureau County, Illinois, Sept. (1848?), Burton Bernard Papers, Lovejoy Library.

16. Celia Ann Lovejoy to Elizabeth Lovejoy, letter, Apr. 10, 1841, Wickett-Wiswall Collection.

17. Burton Bernard, "Remarks at Unveiling of Memorial of Celia Ann Lovejoy," Nov. 9, 1987, Burton Bernard Papers, Lovejoy Library.

18. John Lovejoy to Joseph Lovejoy, letter, Oct. 1, 1838, Wickett-Wiswall Collection.

19. "Letter of Appeal for the Widow and Son of Elijah P. Lovejoy," Ohio State Convention of Abolitionists, 1841, signed by James C. White et al., Illinois State Historical Library.

20. Celia Ann Lovejoy to Elizabeth Lovejoy, letter, Apr. 10, 1841, Wickett-Wiswall Collection.

21. Tanner, *History*, 90.

22. Edward Lovejoy to H. L. Hammond, letter, Mar. 4, 1890, Wickett-Wiswall Collection.

23. Edward Lovejoy to H. L. Hammond, letter, Mar. 4, 1890, Wickett-Wiswall Collection.

24. Edward Lovejoy to H. L. Hammond, letter, Mar. 4, 1890, Wickett-Wiswall Collection.

25. *Weekly Trinity Journal*, Aug. 16, 1873, quoted in William G. Chrystal, "The 'Wabuska Mangler' as a Martyr's Seed: The Strange Story of Edward P. Lovejoy," paper submitted to the Nevada Historical Society, 1993, 8.

26. *Weekly Trinity Journal*, date uncertain, quoted in Chrystal, 8.

27. *Weekly Trinity Journal*, May 9, 1874, quoted in Chrystal, 8–9.

28. Edward Beecher to Owen Lovejoy, letter, Nov. 14, 1837, Lovejoy Papers, William L. Clements Library.

29. Edward Beecher to Zebina Eastman, letter, Apr. 3, 1874, Chicago Historical Society Library Papers.

30. John Anthony Scott, *Woman Against Slavery* (New York: Thomas Crowell, 1978), 67–68.

31. Harris, 94n.

32. Elizabeth Lovejoy to Owen, Elizabeth G., and John Lovejoy, letter, Dec. 1837, undated, Wickett-Wiswall Collection.

33. Joseph C. Lovejoy to Owen Lovejoy, letter, Dec. 7, 1937, Lovejoy Papers, William L. Clements Library.

34. Owen Lovejoy to J. G. Birney, letter, Dec. 9, 1837, Illinois State Historical Library.

35. *Western Citizen*, quoted in Magdol, 73.

36. Abraham Lincoln, quoted in Magdol, 403.

37. Thaddeus Stevens, quoted in Magdol, 405.

38. John Lovejoy to Abraham Lincoln, letter, Sept. 23, 1864, Robert Todd Lincoln Collection, Library of Congress.

39. John Lovejoy to Elizabeth G. Lovejoy, letter, July 12, 1886, Wickett-Wiswall Collection.

40. Mrs. H. L. Hammond to Thomas Dimmock, letter, June 1, 1891, Missouri Historical Society Library.

9. The Nation Is Stirred

1. Herbert Hoover, program at 100th anniversary of death of Lovejoy, Special Collections, Miller Library.

2. Milton Rugoff, *The Beechers* (New York: Harper and Row, 1981), 199.

3. *Liberator*, Dec. 15, 1837.

4. Robert Storment and John Bingham to R. G. Williams, poem, Jan. 7, 1838, Wickett-Wiswall Collection.

5. Poem, *Liberator*, Dec. 22, 1837.

6. *Emancipator* (extra edition), Feb. 12, 1838.

7. *Philadelphia Observer*, quoted in Tanner, *Martyrdom*, 161.

8. *New York American*, quoted in Tanner, *Martyrdom*, 159–60.

9. *Pittsburgh Times*, quoted in Tanner, *Martyrdom*, 162.

10. *Painesville Republican*, quoted in Tanner, *Martyrdom*, 162.

11. *National Gazette*, quoted in *Emancipator*, Nov. 30, 1837.

12. *Boston Cabinet*, quoted in *Memoir*, 330.

13. *New Yorker*, quoted in *Memoir*, 334.

14. *Newark Daily Advertiser*, quoted in *Memoir*, 336.

15. *New York Journal of Commerce*, quoted in *Memoir*, 333.

16. *Boston Daily Advocate*, quoted in *Memoir*, 328.

17. *Boston Atlas*, quoted in *Memoir*, 329.

18. *Columbus Journal and Register*, quoted in *Emancipator*, Dec. 21, 1837.

19. *Massachusetts Spy*, quoted in *Emancipator*, Dec. 7, 1837.

20. *Cincinnati Journal*, quoted in Tanner, *Martyrdom*, 164.

21. *Cumberland Presbyterian*, quoted in *Emancipator* (extra edition), Feb. 12, 1838.

22. *Louisville Journal*, quoted in Tanner, *Martyrdom*, 164.

23. *Louisville Herald*, quoted in Tanner, *Martyrdom*, 165.

24. *St. Louis Commercial Bulletin*, quoted in Tanner, *Martyrdom*, 165.

25. *Caledonian*, quoted in Tanner, *Martyrdom*, 232.

26. *Baltimore Chronicle*, quoted in *Emancipator* (extra edition), Feb. 12, 1838.

27. *Jeffersonville Courier*, quoted in *Emancipator*, Dec. 7, 1837.

28. *New York Observer*, Dec. 2, 1837.

29. *New York Baptist Register*, quoted in *Emancipator*, Dec. 7, 1837.

30. *Missouri Republican*, Nov. 10, 1837.

31. *Missouri Argus*, Nov. 11, 1837.

32. *New York Evening Post*, Nov. 18, 1837.

33. *Illinois State Register and Illinois Advocate*, Nov. 24, 1837.

34. *Alton Telegraph*, Nov. 8, 1837.

35. *Boston Daily Advocate*, quoted in *Memoir*, 328.

36. *Alton Telegraph*, Nov. 29, 1837.

37. *Alton Telegraph*, Dec. 20, 1837.

38. *Peoria Register and North-Western Gazetteer*, quoted in Alton *Observer*, Dec. 28, 1837.

39. *Peoria Register and North-Western Gazetteer*, Dec. 16, 1837.

40. *Northwestern Gazette and Galena Advertiser*, Nov. 18, 1837.

41. Beriah Green, *A Discourse in Commemoration of the Martyrdom of the Rev. Elijah P. Lovejoy* (New York: American Anti-Slavery Society, 1838), 17–18.

42. Thomas Stone, *The Martyr of Freedom. A Discourse*, delivered Nov. 30, 1837 (Boston: Isaac Knapp, 1838), 20.

43. Chester Hardwick, quoted in *Memoir*, 306.

44. Horace Greeley, quoted in *New Yorker*, in Russel Nye, *Fettered Freedom: Civil Liberties and the Slavery Controversy* (East Lansing: Michigan State College Press, 1949), 120.

45. Lincoln, 111–12.

46. *Memoir*, 319.

47. The story is related by Rev. Edward Brown (cousin of John Brown) in Justus Newton Brown, "Lovejoy's Influence on John Brown," *Magazine of History*, Sept.–Oct. 1916.

48. William Herndon, *Herndon's Life of Lincoln*, ed. Paul Angle (New York: World Publishing Co., 1949), 150.

49. Lyman Trumbull to his father, letter, Nov. 12, 1837, quoted in Horace White, *The Life of Lyman Trumbull* (New York: Houghton Mifflin, 1938), 8–10.

50. Edmund Quincy, quoted in Samuel May, *Some Recollections of Our Antislavery Conflict* (Boston: Fields, Osgood, 1869), 229.

51. *Liberator*, Dec. 15, 1837.

52. Wendell Phillips, quoted in *Liberator*, Dec. 15, 1837.

53. *The Freedom Speech of Wendell Phillips* (booklet distributed by the Wendell Phillips Hall Association), ed. John Latham (Boston, 1891), 14–15.

54. Artemus Bowers Muzzey, quoted in *The Freedom Speech of Wendell Phillips*, 5–6.

55. Alvan Stewart, Jan. 10, 1838, quoted in *Memoir*, 362.

56. Feb. 10, 1838, Wickett-Wiswall Collection.

57. Story related by Rev. Edward Brown in Justus Newton Brown.

58. Thomas Ford, *History of Illinois* (Chicago: S. C. Griggs, 1854), 234.

59. John Quincy Adams, quoted in Ford, 238–39.

60. Ralph Waldo Emerson, quoted in John Dunphy, "The Martyrdom of Lovejoy," *Illinois Issues*, Jan.–Feb. 1985.

61. Reid, 71.

62. Melvin Jameson, *Elijah Parish Lovejoy as a Christian* (Rochester, N.Y.: Scranton, Wetmore, 1911), 8.

63. Wendell Phillips to the *Anti-Slavery Standard*, letter written from Alton, Apr. 14, 1867 (reprinted in *Alton Evening Telegraph*).

64. Wendell Phillips, quoted in Jameson, 110–14.

65. Tanner, *Martyrdom*, 8.

66. *Reminiscences of Hon. S. V. White* (Brooklyn: Daily Eagle, 1900), 12, Illinois State Historical Library.

67. Nelson Miles Heikes, "Sketch of the Life of Rev. Elijah Parish Lovejoy" (pamphlet), published by the Ladies of the Grand Army of the Republic of Albion, Maine.

68. J. M. Wilkerson, quoted in *Dedication of the Lovejoy Monument* (Alton: Charles Holden, 1897), 19.

Postscript

1. Elijah Lovejoy, quoted in *Liberator*, Nov. 10, 1837.

2. Martin Luther King, Jr., "Letter from Birmingham Jail," Apr. 16, 1963, Library of Congress.

3. Samuel Willard, quoted in Tanner, *Martyrdom*, 216–17.

Index

Paul Simon represents Illinois in the United States Senate. For eighteen years, he was a newspaper publisher in Madison County, Illinois, where Alton is located. He is also the author of fourteen previous books.